Grade 3

Jumbo Workbook

This workbook belongs to

You will need the stickers and press-out cards at the back to complete some activities. Where a sticker is missing, you will usually see this pattern.

Dear Parents,

Welcome to the *Grade 3 Jumbo Workbook*!

Grade 3 can feel like a big step up from grade 2, especially in math, where children work with multiplication and division for the first time. Here are some tips to help your child consolidate the concepts learned in school.

★ Look at the pages with your child, ensuring he or she knows what to do before starting.

★ Plan short, regular sessions, only doing one or two pages at a time.

★ Praise your child's efforts and persistence.

★ Encourage your child to assess his or her own efforts in a positive way. For example, say: "I like the way you redid the ones you got wrong. That'll help you remember how to do these problems."

★ Make the learning sessions positive experiences. Give prompts where they might help. If a section is too hard for your child, leave those pages until he or she is ready for them.

★ Relate the learning to things in your child's world. For example, discuss the fractions of food already eaten in a cake, pizza, or candy bar.

★ At the back of the book is an answer section. Encourage your child to attempt the activities and check them over before looking at the answers. Some activities have open questions with no right or wrong answer. Help your child to recognize these activities and to use self-expression.

Together, the activities in this workbook help build a solid understanding of core learning concepts and topics to ensure your child is ready for fourth grade.

We wish your child hours of enjoyment with this fun workbook!

Scholastic Early Learning

Picture credits: All photos courtesy of **Shutterstock**, unless noted as follows: **David F. Barry/Wikimedia Commons:** 231br (Sitting Bull); **Dennis van de Water/ Shutterstock.com:** 95tr (The Louvre); **erkanatbas/Shutterstock.com:** 181tml (blue and silver car); **Hendrickson Photography/Shutterstock.com:** 223ml (St. Louis Gateway Arch); **Johnnie Rik/Shutterstock.com:** 49bmr (blue car); **neftali/Shutterstock.com:** 231mr (Crazy Horse); **OlegRi/Shutterstock.com:** 49mr (red motorcycle); **vectormall/Shutterstock.com:** 21bc (Martin Luther King, Jr.).

Contents

The Main Idea

The **main idea** is the topic that covers the whole text. A **summary** is an overview that includes the main idea of each paragraph but not the details.

Read the text, and then complete the activities below.

Honeybees are important insects because they help plants grow. They carry tiny yellow grains called pollen between flowers. This process is called pollination. It allows plants to produce seeds that then grow into new plants. A great deal of our food comes from plants that rely on pollination. Without bees, we would have less to eat.

Sadly, bees are under threat. Human activities such as farming are replacing the wildflowers bees need. We also use chemicals called pesticides on our crops. Some of them kill bees.

How can we help? If you have a backyard, plant plenty of flowers, and don't spray them with chemicals. If you see a bee lying on the ground, it may need food. Try giving it a drop of white sugar mixed with water to help it on its way. Remember, never feed bees honey. You might pass on a bee disease.

1 Write a title for this text that explains the main idea.

_____

2 Write a short summary of this text. Remember to include the main idea of each paragraph.

_____

_____

_____

_____

_____

_____

The Details

The **details** are pieces of information that explain or support the main idea.

Reread the text on page 4. Then read the sentences below. Put a **check mark** by the details that are in the text. Put an **X** by the details that are not in the text.

Harmful chemicals called pesticides are killing bees.

Bees transport pollen between flowers.

Honeybees live in hives made up of thousands of insects.

A bee lying on the ground may need food.

Honeybees tell one another where to find food by doing a waggle dance.

Choose another detail from each paragraph, and write it in a box below.

1 _____

_____

2 _____

_____

3 _____

_____

The Plot

The **plot** is the main sequence of events in a story. It has three parts that usually follow this order: beginning, climax, and ending.

Draw lines to match each sentence to the correct story part.

The story's setting, characters, and main conflict or problem are introduced.

beginning

The problem is fully resolved and the story ends.

climax

This is the story's most exciting moment. It's when the main character faces their biggest problem.

ending

Read this Chinese fairy tale, and then name the parts of the plot structure.

Long ago, a young girl called Ye Xian lived in a cave village with her wicked stepmother and horrible stepsister. Ye Xian's stepfamily were jealous of her kindness and beauty. They bullied her and made her do the hardest jobs. When it was time for the New Year Festival, Ye Xian's stepfamily would not let her go. Sad and lonely, she stayed at home cleaning. _____

Suddenly, the spirit of a magical fish appeared. It granted Ye Xian's wishes and sent her to the festival in a beautiful dress and golden slippers. Everyone at the festival admired Ye Xian's dress and slippers. She had a wonderful time until she saw her stepmother and stepsister. Terrified that they would recognize her, Ye Xian ran away, leaving one golden slipper behind. _____

A local king bought the slipper from a merchant and set out to find the shoe's owner. When he came to Ye Xian's house, her stepsister tried to squeeze a big foot into the delicate slipper. It didn't fit. Then Ye Xian tried on the slipper. It fit perfectly. She left her horrible stepfamily for the king's home, where they lived happily ever after. _____

Reread the fairy tale on page 6. Then answer the questions in each box to complete the story roller coaster.

Who is the main character in the story?

_____

Where is the story set?

_____

What is the main problem?

_____

_____

_____

_____

What is the most exciting moment?

_____

_____

How does the main character face her problem?

_____

_____

_____

How is the problem resolved?

_____

_____

_____

_____

_____

_____

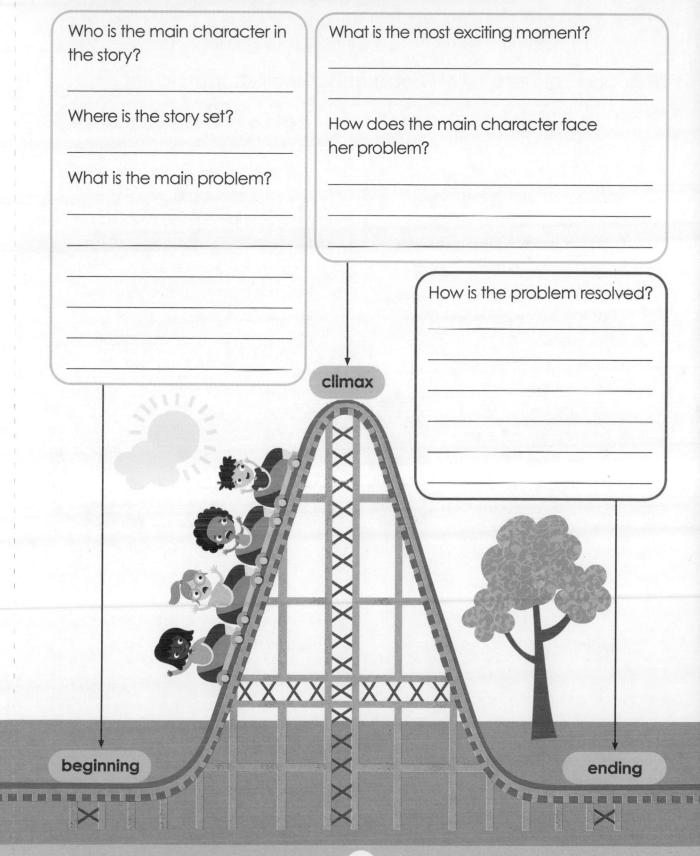

climax

beginning

ending

Characters

Feelings such as excitement are temporary. They change with the situation. Traits such as kindness or selfishness don't change as quickly.

Luke and Lola are twins. Read about their school days.

Lola stomped into school with a scowl. She didn't cheer up until recess, when she found the cookies her mom had packed. Then she noticed that her friend Beth had already taken a cookie. Lola was happy to share, but right then she was angry.

"Ask before you take my food!" she snapped.

"I'm sorry," Beth replied. "I'll ask next time."

Lola forgave her, and they shared the cookies. Then it was time for math. Lola smiled. She liked solving tricky problems.

Luke bounced out of bed. Today his class was going to the zoo!

The journey was long, however, and Luke was soon bored. When they finally arrived, the class split into groups. Luke noticed that the new girl, Mia, didn't have a group.

Without thinking, he called out, "Mia, come and join our group!"

At lunchtime, Luke couldn't find his lunch. He wasn't surprised, because he often forgot things, but he was worried that he'd be hungry.

"Don't worry," Mia said. "I've got a huge lunch. Let's share!"

Use the word stickers from the back of the book to complete the chart.

Lola		Luke	
feelings	traits	feelings	traits

Setting

The **setting** is when and where a story takes place. Writers often include details such as time, weather, or what characters see, hear, and feel.

Read this story opening, and then answer the questions below.

The cobbled London streets slept under a jet-black sky. A few gas lanterns flickered as a strong gust of wind whistled past, disturbing piles of fallen leaves. Thunder rumbled in the distance and the occasional drop of rain fell.

The tall man shivered and pulled his long dark coat closer around him. As he crept along the street, he remembered to keep to the shadows. Quickly, he ducked into a narrow doorway and pulled out an old brass pocket watch. He saw the hands tick over to midnight, then repocketed the watch and hurried on his way.

1 Where is this story set?

_____

2 What time of day is it?

_____

3 In about what time in the past is this story set?

_____

4 Underline four words that describe the weather.

5 Choose your own setting and write a few sentences to describe it.

_____

_____

_____

_____

_____

Types of Language

Literal language means exactly what it says. Figurative language means something other than what is written. It can make writing more interesting.

Color the box **blue** if the phrase in *italics* is literal.
Color the box **orange** if the phrase in *italics* is figurative.

Gabriel put on his headphones and *danced around his bedroom.*

Emily couldn't keep her secret, so she *spilled the beans* to Madison.

The *car's engine grumbled* as Mr. Smith turned the key in the ignition.

Isabelle was so hungry *she could have eaten an elephant.*

Jacob ripped the packet and *spilled the beans* all over the floor.

Logan finished his test quickly because it was *a piece of cake.*

The icy air was filled with *dancing snowflakes.*

Cameron's smile was *a mile wide.*

Grace ate *a piece of cake* at her surprise birthday party.

Personification is giving an animal or object human traits. Hyperbole is exaggeration. Idioms are common phrases using figurative language.

Read the sentences in the boxes you colored orange. Write an **I** by the sentences that contain idioms, a **P** by those that use personification, and an **H** by those that use hyperbole.

Similes and Metaphors

A **metaphor** compares two things by saying they are the same thing.
A **simile** compares two things using words such as **like** or **as**.

Read each metaphor, and then rewrite it as a simile.

The dancer was a graceful swan on the stage.

The dancer glided like a swan across the stage.

The baby was an angel all day.

_____

Mrs. Jenkins was a simmering volcano, ready to explode.

_____

Write a simile and a metaphor for each word pair below.

brain / computer

_____

_____

voice / nightingale

_____

_____

stars / diamonds

_____

_____

lake / mirror

_____

_____

Cause and Effect

A **cause** is the reason why something happens. The **effect** is what happens.

For each cause below, circle the picture that shows a likely effect.

One day, during summer vacation, Carlos went into his backyard. After about ten minutes, he felt too hot to continue playing.

Alice walked along the river with her dog, Rover. Suddenly, Rover jumped into the river. When he climbed out, he gave himself a great big shake.

Mom was driving home from work when her car's engine made a strange noise. A few minutes later, the car rumbled to a stop.

Isaac planted some flower seeds in a big pot. He put them in a sunny spot on the windowsill and watered them every week for a few months.

Fables

A **fable** is a short story that teaches us a lesson, or moral.
Fables often have talking animals as characters.

Long ago, a Greek man named Aesop wrote many fables.
Read one of his fables below, and then answer the questions.

The Fox and the Stork

A sly fox was always laughing at a stork's odd appearance. He decided to play a trick on the stork.

"You must have dinner with me today," he said to the stork.

The stork accepted the invitation and arrived at the fox's home with a big appetite. The fox served soup in a shallow dish, and all the stork could do was wet the tip of her beak. The fox laughed at the stork and slurped his soup easily.

The hungry stork was upset, but she didn't get angry. Instead, she said to the fox, "You must eat dinner with me tomorrow."

When the fox arrived at the stork's house, he smelled a delicious fish dinner. However, the dinner was served in a tall jar with a narrow neck. The stork could reach the food with her long beak, but the fox could only lick the outside of the jar. He flew into a wild rage, while the stork calmly ate her dinner.

1 Why did the fox want to play a trick on the stork?

2 Why do you think the stork chose not to get angry at the fox?

3 What do you think is the lesson, or moral, of this story?

Myths

A **myth** is an ancient story told by a culture to explain natural events or its beliefs and practices.

Read this Norse myth, and then answer the questions below.

The goddess Idun lived with the other gods in Asgard. She kept a basket of golden apples, which the gods ate to stay young forever.

One day, the god of mischief, Loki, fought with the giant Thiazi. To stop the quarrel, Loki promised to kidnap Idun for the giant. He lured Idun into a trap, and Thiazi stole her away to Jotunheim, the land of the giants.

Soon, the gods began to age. They discovered Loki was to blame, and forced him to choose between fetching Idun or paying with his life.

Loki transformed into a falcon and flew to Jotunheim. He turned Idun into a nut and set off with her grasped in his claws. When Thiazi found Idun missing, he became an eagle and chased Loki.

Loki raced back to Asgard, flying faster than ever before. As soon as he arrived, the other gods set a fire outside the city walls. Thiazi was flying too fast to stop. He flew into the fire, setting his feathers alight. He fell to the ground, defeated. This is how the Norse gods kept the power of eternal youth.

1 What choice did the gods give Loki?

_____

_____

2 Why do you think they forced him to make this choice?

_____

_____

3 What ancient belief does this myth explain?

_____

_____

4 Write three adjectives to describe Loki.

_____

Folktales

A **folktale** is an old story told by a culture. In the past, most people couldn't read or write, so stories were passed down by word of mouth.

Read this folktale from the Indigenous people of present-day Alabama. Then answer the questions below.

In the beginning, Fire was owned by Bear. Bear carried Fire with her wherever she went. One day, Bear came to a huge forest with a floor covered in tasty acorns. Bear set Fire down at the forest's edge and began to wander far away from Fire, eating the acorns as she went.

Fire began to run out of wood. "**Feed me! Feed me!**" he cried, but Bear had wandered too far to hear him. Soon, a human came along and found that Fire had almost died out.

"**Can I help?**" he asked Fire.

"**Please bring me sticks and twigs to eat,**" said Fire.

The human did as Fire asked, and soon Fire was burning brightly again. The human enjoyed Fire's warmth, and they were happy together. When Bear finally returned, Fire was angry and chased her away. This is why Fire now belongs to humans, not bears.

1 Write two examples of personification used to describe the bear and the fire.

_____

_____

2 Why do you think many people still enjoy folktales today?

_____

_____

_____

3 Find and read a local folktale. Write a short summary of the story here.

_____

_____

_____

Poems About Nature

Poets often use images of nature to write about their feelings and ideas.

Read this poem by Christina Rossetti, and then answer the questions below.

Who has seen the wind?
    Neither I nor you.
But when the leaves hang trembling,
    The wind is passing through.

Who has seen the wind?
    Neither you nor I.
But when the trees bow down their heads,
    The wind is passing by.

1 Which line is repeated exactly in the first and second stanzas?

_____

2 Why do you think the poet repeats this line?

_____

_____

3 Write two examples of personification used in this poem.

_____

_____

4 A poem's stanzas have different names depending on their length. Circle the name for the stanzas in this poem.

couplet (2 lines)   tercet (3 lines)   quatrain (4 lines)

5 Read the poem again. Circle the two adjectives you think this poet would use to describe the wind.

mysterious   beautiful   happy   funny   powerful   lazy

Limericks

Limericks are 5-line poems. Lines 1, 2, and 5 rhyme with one another, and lines 3 and 4 also rhyme. Limericks are often funny or nonsensical.

Read this limerick by Edward Lear, and then complete the activities below.

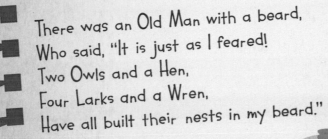

There was an Old Man with a beard,
Who said, "It is just as I feared!
Two Owls and a Hen,
Four Larks and a Wren,
Have all built their nests in my beard."

1   Look at the words at the ends of the lines. Underline each set of rhyming words using different colored pencils.

2   Why do you think this poem is nonsensical?

_____

_____

Fill in the blank spaces to finish your own limerick. Remember to use the correct rhyming pattern.

There once was a young girl _____

Who _____

She _____

And _____

Then _____.

Fact Versus Opinion

Facts are true statements that we can prove.
Opinions are people's views, beliefs, or feelings about something.

Read this ad for the opening of a new ice-cream store. Write an **F** by the statements that are facts. Write an **O** by those that are opinions.

Brand-New Ice-Cream Store!

Come and try the tastiest ice cream in town! ☐

We open on Saturday at 11:00 a.m. ☐

We have more than 50 flavors on sale. ☐

Kids will love building their own sundaes. ☐

Once you try our ice cream, you'll never buy another brand again. ☐

One scoop costs $1.99. ☐

Two scoops cost $2.99. ☐

Get a free topping with your first purchase. ☐

Point of View

A writer's point of view is their opinion or belief on a topic.

Read the text, and then answer the questions below.

Are Books Better Than Movies?

I prefer reading books to watching movies. When I read fiction, I picture the characters and setting in my mind. Movies stop people from being creative because they already see everything happening on screen.

Also, books are much more detailed than movies. Directors often turn books into movies that are less than two hours long. This means that they miss out a great deal of important information. In my opinion, this ruins the story.

Finally, reading is a better way to relax before going to sleep than watching movies. Screens emit blue light, which tricks your body into thinking it is daytime. This makes it more difficult to go to sleep. Not getting enough sleep is bad for your health, so I always choose to read before bed. I think everyone should read more books instead of watching movies.

1 Does the writer think that books are better than movies?
Circle the correct answer. **Yes / No**

2 Circle the writer's three supporting reasons using different colored pencils.

3 Write three arguments you would make if you were disagreeing with the writer's point of view.

1 _____

_____

2 _____

_____

3 _____

_____

Step-by-Step Instructions

Step-by-step instructions tell people how to do something.
The instructions are in the order people use them.

The instructions below are in the wrong order. Write the missing step numbers to show the correct order. Use the diagrams to help you.

Make a Paper Plane

You will need:
- a sheet of construction paper

1 Fold the piece of paper in half lengthways. Then open it out again.

5 Now fold the outer edge over to make a wing.

Fold points A and B in so they meet in the middle.

Fold the plane in half so the edges line up.

Turn the plane over and repeat step 5.

Hold your plane under the wings. Then launch it into the air.

Fold the top two corners in so they meet in the middle.

Follow the steps in the correct order to make your own paper plane.

Biographies

A **biography** is a description of a real person's life.

Read this short biography. Then complete the timeline of Martin Luther King, Jr.'s life.

Martin Luther King, Jr.
(1929–1968)

Martin Luther King, Jr. was a key leader of the American civil rights movement. This movement was an ongoing fight for equal rights for African Americans.

King was born in 1929 in Atlanta. He was clever and started college in 1944 at just 15 years old. In 1955, he helped to organize the Montgomery Bus Boycott. During this yearlong boycott, African Americans didn't use public transportation. They were protesting the unfair laws separating Black and white people on city buses. The successful boycott ended when Montgomery officials got rid of this law.

King was also a powerful speaker. In 1963, he joined the March on Washington. Around 250,000 people met by the Lincoln Memorial in Washington, D.C., where King gave his famous "I Have a Dream" speech.

One year later, he won the Nobel Peace Prize for his work on civil rights. At the time, he was the youngest person to win this impressive prize.

King died in 1968 when he was killed at a protest in Memphis.

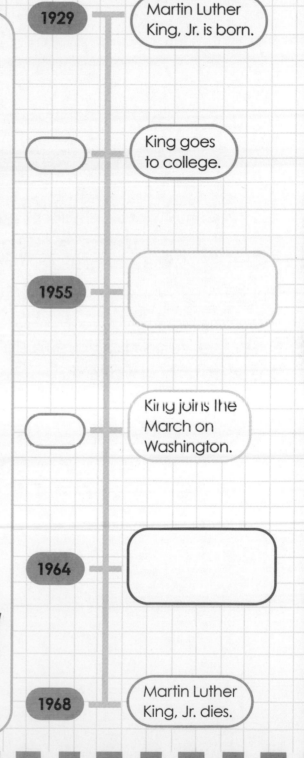

1929 — Martin Luther King, Jr. is born.

⬭ — King goes to college.

1955 —

⬭ — King joins the March on Washington.

1964 —

1968 — Martin Luther King, Jr. dies.

Compare and Contrast

When we **compare** texts, we find **similarities** and **differences** between them.

Read Text 1 on page 22 and Text 2 on page 23.

Text 1

January 19, 2023

Dear Principal Wilkins,

We think the new school uniform policy is a bad idea. There are many reasons for this.

First, wearing school uniforms will take away our freedom. Students want to express themselves with their clothes. If everyone wears the same thing, we'll lose this chance to be creative.

Also, although the uniforms are neat, they are uncomfortable. We can't concentrate well in school if we have to wear uncomfortable clothes every day.

Finally, the new school uniforms are expensive. Our parents shouldn't have to spend this extra money when we already have clothes at home.

Therefore, please consider changing the decision to make us all wear school uniforms. We will all benefit.

Yours sincerely,

Mrs. Andersen's class

Fill in the Venn diagram to show the **differences** and **similarities** between the two texts.

Text 1   **Text 2**

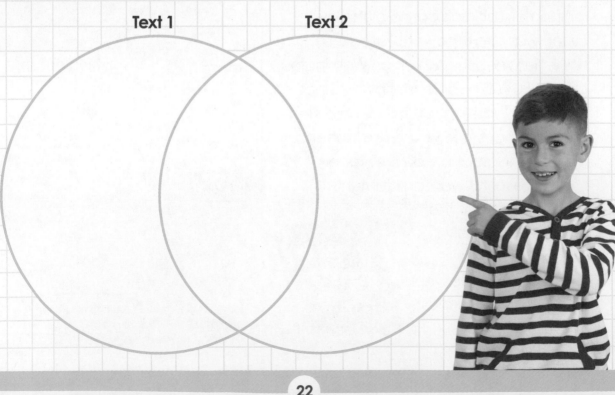

To **compare and contrast** two texts, think about factors such as genre, the author's purpose, the intended reader, and the subject matter.

Text 2   January 24, 2023

Elementary School Adopts New Uniform Policy

By Lucy Brown

Students at Oak Hill Elementary School will start wearing uniforms. The new uniform will be the same for boys and girls—a white shirt, black blazer, dress pants, and a tie in the school's colors of blue and yellow.

Most staff are happy with the decision. Principal Wilkins said, "The policy will improve our school's reputation. The new uniforms are neat, and wearing them will make all students feel equal. They'll also remove the pressure of deciding what to wear every morning."

However, not all students agree.

One class wrote to their principal, arguing against the decision. They suggest that the uniforms are too expensive. Part of the letter reads, "Our parents shouldn't have to spend extra money when we already have clothes at home."

The new policy will be introduced from next Monday morning.

Reread both texts, and then answer the questions below.

1 Circle the genre for Text 1 in **red** and the genre for Text 2 in green.

letter   book report   email   blog   newspaper article   journal entry

2 What do you think was the author's purpose for writing Text 1?

_____

_____

3 What do you think was the author's purpose for writing Text 2?

_____

_____

4 Which text presents both sides of the argument about school uniforms, and which is more one-sided?

_____

_____

Build a Paragraph

A **paragraph** is a group of sentences that share one main idea.

How to Build a Paragraph

1 Write a topic sentence that introduces the main idea.

2 Add details that support the idea.

3 Finish with a concluding statement that sums up the topic.

topic sentence

detail

detail

detail

concluding statement

Read the text. Underline the topic sentence in **blue**, the details in **red**, and the concluding statement in **green**.

Tyrannosaurus rex was one of the fiercest dinosaurs on Earth. It hunted other animals, which means it was a predator. *T. rex* also had a huge body that could grow up to 40 feet long. That's about as long as a school bus! Each one of *T. rex's* sharp teeth was the size of a banana. This is why *T. rex* was called "king of the tyrant lizards."

Put a **check** by the paragraph's missing topic sentence.

You need a great deal of energy and skill to play this game, but it is also fun. My favorite position is pitcher, because I am good at throwing the ball. Yesterday, I played a game, and I hit a home run. Next year, I hope to become the captain of my school team.

☐ My favorite sport is soccer.

☐ My favorite sport is basketball.

☐ My favorite sport is baseball.

Write a Paragraph

Write notes about your favorite season and why you like it.

Topic: _____
_____

Detail 1: _____
_____

Detail 2: _____
_____

Detail 3: _____
_____

Conclusion: _____
_____

Use your notes to write a paragraph.

Add Details

Good writers add **details** to their sentences that answer the questions who, when, why, where, and how.

Write the question word that is answered by the **bold** words or phrases in each sentence.

He traveled **to Europe**.   where

I ran **to catch the bus**.   _____

The **little baby** crawled.   _____

They played **all morning**.   _____

She sang **angelically**.   _____

Rewrite the sentences below, adding more details.

The dog sat.
The white dog sat on the bedroom rug.

He went outside.

_____

We ate.

_____

She arrived.

_____

The teacher talked.

_____

I slept.

_____

Fiction Genres

We group fiction texts in categories, or **genres**, such as mystery or humor.

Add stickers to match the book covers to the correct genres.

The Hare and the Tortoise

Collected Funny Tales

Aliens on Mars

The Case of the Missing Jewels

Little Unicorn's Journey

Treasure Island

Name a story genre that you enjoy reading. On the next few pages, you'll plan a story in that genre.

_____

Create Characters

Fill in the profiles on pages 28 and 29 to create two characters for your story.

Character's name:

_____

Age:

_____

Draw your character in this box.

Where and when does your character live?

_____

_____

_____

List three character traits, such as *kind*, *funny*, or *scared*.

1 _____

2 _____

3 _____

What does your character want most of all?

_____

_____

_____

Choose one of the character traits, and describe why this trait may change because of the events in the story.

_____

_____

_____

_____

Create Characters

Good writers build relationships between characters to make them seem real.

Character's name:

_____

Age:

_____

Draw your character in this box.

Where and when does your character live?

_____

_____

_____

List three character traits, such as *kind, funny,* or *scared.*

1 _____

2 _____

3 _____

What does your character want most of all?

_____

_____

Imagine your characters know each other. Are they friends or enemies? How do they act around each other?

_____

_____

_____

_____

Create a Setting

Choose a setting for a story featuring the characters you created on pages 28 and 29. Write short notes about it here.

The place is _____

_____

They can hear _____

_____

They might taste _____

_____

My characters can see _____

_____

They can smell _____

_____

They might feel _____

_____

Draw a picture of your setting here.

Use your notes to write a description of the setting.

_____

_____

_____

_____

_____

Story Openings

A good **story opening** grabs readers' attention and makes them want to keep reading.

Draw lines to join the starting strategies to the story openings.

Start with action or dialogue.	I'm Henry, and I am 8 years old.
Describe the setting.	I turned my room upside down, but I couldn't find my homework anywhere.
Let your main character introduce themselves.	The old, creaky mansion stood on the hill for more than 100 years.
Ask a question.	"Oh no!" Katy cried. "What have you done now?"
Introduce a problem.	Can you keep a secret?

Choose one or more of the starting strategies, and use the picture as a prompt to write your own story opening.

Time Machine

Write an Ending

A good ending solves the problem in a story.

Read the story, and then answer the questions below.

"Quick!" shouted Ava. "Pass me the ball."
Liam kicked the ball in Ava's direction. Everyone watched as it soared over her head and landed in a patch of trees beyond the park fence.

"That's my brother's ball," Caleb said. "We have to find it."

The children climbed over the fence and began to search. They found the ball a few minutes later, but it soon lay forgotten as they chased one another through the wood.

After a while, Ava's stomach rumbled. "Let's go home for lunch," she called.

The friends looked around, but all they could see were trees in every direction. Not one of them could remember the way back to the park.

1 What is the unsolved problem in this story?

_____

2 How might the problem be solved? Who could solve it?

_____

_____

3 Write an ending for this story that solves the problem.

_____

_____

_____

_____

_____

Plan a Story

Good writers often make a **plan** to organize their ideas before they begin writing their story.

Write a plan for your story. Use the genre, characters, and setting you chose on the previous pages, but make any changes that might improve the story.

Story title

_____

Genre

_____

Setting

Time: _____

Place: _____

Main characters

Character 1: _____

Character 2: _____

Other characters

_____

_____

What is the main problem in the story?

_____

How do your main characters face this problem?

_____

_____

How is the problem resolved?

_____

_____

How do your characters learn a lesson or change by the story's end?

_____

_____

Write a Draft

A **rough draft** is the first version of a piece of writing. Writers edit and rewrite their draft before it is published.

Write a draft of the story you planned on page 33.

Story title: _____

_____

_____

_____

_____

_____

_____

_____

_____

_____

_____

_____

_____

_____

_____

_____

_____

_____

_____

_____

Practice Editing

Writers **edit** their work to correct the mistakes
and get it ready for publication.

Read the text, and then complete the editing checklist. Put a
check mark by each instruction once you've completed it.

My Perfect Day

Last saturday, I had the best day ever I woke up later than usaul because I didn't have to get up for school.

Would you like pancakes for breakfast Dad asked.

Pancakes are my best favorite breakfast, so I shouted Yes! as quickly as I could.

After breakfst, Mom took me to the park to meet my friends, harry and amelia. we played socer and Frisbee, and we went on the swings. i swung up as high as I could, and it felt like I was flying.

We played for hours and hours Then we all had an ice cream because we were hot and tired. I chose mint choc chip flava and Mom let me have too scoops.

When we got bak from the park, i watched a hilarious funny movie with my little younger brother. My brther and I laughed so much that our stomuks hurt.

That night, I went to bed with a big smile on my face because I'd had such an awesum wonderful day

Editing Checklist

- Circle incorrect spellings in **red**. ☐

- Underline missing capital letters in **green**. ☐

- Add missing punctuation (periods, question marks, exclamation marks, and commas) in **blue**. ☐

- Add missing speech marks in **orange**. ☐

- Cross out unnecessary words in **purple**. ☐

Write a Final Version

Writers make a **final version** of their story using their draft and making changes to improve it.

Write a final version of your story here. Include the title.

_____

_____

_____

_____

_____

_____

_____

_____

_____

_____

_____

Draw a picture to go with it.

_____

_____

_____

_____

_____

_____

_____

_____

_____

Write a Book Report

A book report includes facts about a story, such as its characters, setting, and plot. It also includes the reader's opinion of the book.

Write a report on a book you have read recently.

Title: _____

Author: _____

Genre: _____

Main characters: _____

_____

Setting: _____

_____

Plot: What are the main events in the story?

_____

_____

_____

_____

Opinion: Did you enjoy the book? Why?

_____

_____

_____

_____

_____

Recommendation: Would you recommend this book to others? Why?

_____

_____

_____

_____

Write a Persuasive Text

Writers of **persuasive** texts try to make readers agree with their point of view. They include reasons to support their opinion.

For each statement, circle agree or disagree, and then list three supporting reasons for your opinion.

Junk food should be banned in schools.

I agree / disagree.

1 _____

2 _____

3 _____

Everyone should recycle.

I agree / disagree.

1 _____

2 _____

3 _____

Writers use **linking words** and **phrases** to connect their opinions and reasons. They use words such as *also, because, therefore, since,* and *for example.*

Read the text. Then circle the linking words and phrases.

In my opinion, cats make better pets than dogs. First, cats are easier to take care of. For example, they can wash and exercise themselves. You must walk a dog at least twice a day. Therefore, dogs take up more of your time than cats.

Also, cats are much less annoying than dogs because their meow is quite quiet. Dogs often bark loudly, which might disturb your neighbors.

Since cats enjoy being alone, you can leave them at home while you go to school. Cats are great companions, but they need less attention than dogs. For these reasons, I think that a cat is a better choice for a pet than a dog.

Write a Persuasive Text

Think of a topic you feel strongly about. Write short notes about it here.

Opinion: _____

Reason 1: _____

Reason 2: _____

Reason 3: _____

Conclusion: _____

_____

Use your notes to write a persuasive text. Remember to use linking words and phrases to connect your opinion with your reasons.

_____
_____
_____
_____
_____
_____
_____
_____
_____
_____
_____
_____

Write a Letter

A formal **letter** has five parts: address, greeting, body, closing, and signature.

Read Mason's letter to his grandma. Then sticker the labels to name the parts of the letter.

43 Green Avenue
Mill City
February 8, 2023

Dear Grandma,

Thank you so much for the toy cars you sent me for my birthday. Emma and I have already had lots of fun racing them around the backyard.

On Saturday, my friends are coming to our house. They are bringing their cars, and we're going to have a racing tournament. I can't wait!

Your grandson,

Mason Peters

Write a thank you letter to someone you know. Remember to include all the parts of a formal letter.

_____ ,

_____

_____

_____

_____

_____

_____ ,

_____

Write a Poem

An **acrostic poem** uses the letters of a topic word to start each line of the poem. Each line then describes the topic word.

Write a letter at the start of each line to find the topic word.

- treaks of lightning flash in the sky.

- hunder rumbles far away.

- ver the horizon, clouds roll in.

- ain thuds on the ground.

- onstrous winds rip through the trees.

Choose a topic word, and then write your own acrostic poem.

Draw a picture to go with your poem.

Know About Nouns

A **noun** is a naming word. Most nouns are things that you could see in a picture, such as a **person** or **other living thing**, a **place**, or an **object**.

Underline the two nouns in each sentence. Then rewrite the sentence, replacing the nouns with different ones.

1 We bought <u>food</u> for our <u>cat</u>.

<u>We bought toys for our dog.</u>

2 I dream of riding to France on my skateboard.

_____

3 We saw some huge waves at the beach.

_____

4 I picked some daisies for Mom.

_____

5 He found his phone under the table.

_____

6 The children ate all my favorite candy.

_____

7 He glued glitter on his picture.

_____

8 I'd like the spaghetti and some soda, please.

_____

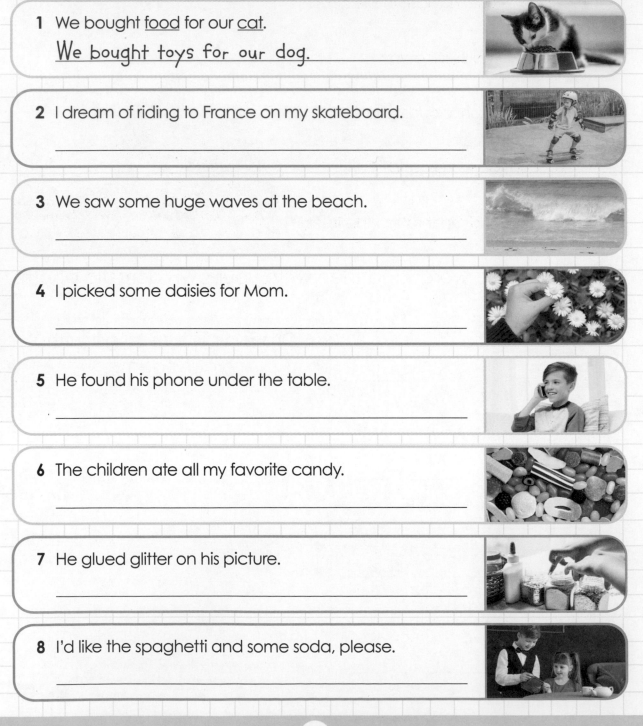

Proper Nouns

Proper nouns are the names of **particular** people, places, brands, days, or events. They always start with a capital letter.

Place the nouns on the sticker sheet in the correct columns. Then add three more words to each side of the chart.

Proper Nouns	Improper Nouns
Sunday	sundae

Plural Nouns

Most **regular nouns** form their plural by adding -s or -es. If they end in -y, the plural ends with -ies. **Irregular nouns** form plurals in other ways.

Regular nouns ending in -s, -ch, -sh, and -x, form their plural by adding -es. Write the plural of each word.

one wish	two __wishes__	one dish	two _____
one bus	two _____	one match	two _____
one kiss	two _____	one box	two _____
one glass	two _____	one peach	two _____

Drop the -y and add -ies to form these plurals.

one baby	two __babies__	one city	two _____
one pony	two _____	one sky	two _____

Correct these irregular plurals. If you don't know an answer, look in a dictionary.

one mouse	two ~~mouses~~ __mice__	one woman	two ~~womans~~ _____
one loaf	two ~~loafs~~ _____	one tooth	two ~~tooths~~ _____
one child	two ~~childs~~ _____	one goose	two ~~gooses~~ _____
one oasis	two ~~oasises~~ _____	one foot	two ~~foots~~ _____
one leaf	two ~~leafs~~ _____	one ox	two ~~oxes~~ _____

Possessive Nouns

Possessive nouns tell you who **owns** something. For singular nouns, add an apostrophe and then an -s (his cat → his cat's tail).

Add the missing apostrophe and the letter -s to each possessive noun.

the bird**'s** tail	the man_ foot
the girl_ laugh	the tree_ roots
the house_ roof	Lucy_ bike

Rewrite each sentence to include a possessive noun.

1 My older sister wears shoes that belong to Mom.
<u>My older sister wears Mom's shoes.</u>

2 I'm looking for the leash that belongs to the dog.
_____

3 I'm staying at the house that belongs to my grandmother.
_____

4 The deck of the ship was battered by the waves.
_____

5 The title of the book is *Pirate Adventure*.
_____

6 We laughed at all the jokes Mateo told.
_____

Possessive Nouns

For plural nouns that end in -s, add an apostrophe (his cats → his cats' tails).
For plural nouns that don't end in -s, add an apostrophe and an -s.

Add the missing apostrophe to each plural noun ending in -s.

the flowers' smell	the babies_ toys
the dogs_ dinners	the rabbits_ hutch
the Wilsons_ house	the bananas_ skins

Add the missing apostrophe and -s to each plural noun.

the cacti's spines	the fish__ tails
the geese__ feathers	the people__ bags
the children__ lunch	the fishermen__ boats

Rewrite each sentence using a possessive noun.

1 Are you looking for the house belonging to the Millers?

<u>Are you looking for the Millers' house?</u>

2 I met Emilia in the waiting room of the dentists.

_____

3 Where is the changing room for women?

_____

4 The caps of the fungi are red with white spots.

_____

Subject Pronouns

Subject pronouns can take the place of the main noun, or the subject of the sentence. *I, you, she, he, it, we,* and *they* are subject pronouns.

Circle the subject pronoun in each sentence.

1 This morning, (I) had cereal for breakfast.

2 You are the fastest runner in our class.

3 They don't believe me.

4 It is hiding in the forest.

5 Yesterday, we went to an amusement park.

6 She is looking forward to her birthday.

Rewrite the sentences replacing the **bold** words with subject pronouns.

1 **Landon** gave Grace and Charlie a turn on his bike.
<u>He gave Grace and Charlie a turn on his bike.</u>

2 **Maddie and I** are playing a computer game.
_____

3 **The Turners** are away on vacation.
_____

4 **That coat** is brand new.
_____

5 **Penny** wants to buy the next book in the series.
_____

Object Pronouns

Object pronouns can take the place of a noun that the subject does something to. *Me, you, her, him, it, us,* and *them* are object pronouns.

Circle the object pronoun in each sentence.

1 I helped (him) clean the car.

2 Our teacher read us a funny story.

3 Caden told her the secret.

4 We put it back on the shelf.

5 The alien stared at me.

6 I'll give you a call tomorrow.

Rewrite the sentences replacing the **bold** words with object pronouns.

1 Abby took **Luna** home from school.

   Abby took her home from school.

2 Dad hid **the gift** in his closet.

   _____

3 I talked to **Leah and Henry**.

   _____

4 We gave **Julian** a surprise party.

   _____

5 The rain soaked **Maia and me**.

   _____

Possessive Adjectives

Possessive adjectives go in front of nouns, telling readers who owns what. My, your, his, her, its, our, and their are possessive adjectives.

Circle the possessive adjective or adjectives in each sentence.

1 They found (their) lost tickets.

2 My house is across the road.

3 We gave our dog a new collar.

4 Tom put his hands in his pockets.

5 She left her bag at my place.

6 Don't lose your mouse in our house.

Rewrite the sentences replacing the **bold** words with possessive adjectives.

1 I like **that man's** motorcycle.

   I like his motorcycle.

2 I found **Grandma's** missing false teeth.

   _____

3 That's **the Lopez's** blue car.

   _____

4 I saw **the ship's** mast swaying in the wind.

   _____

5 I wish I had **that girl's** bravery.

   _____

Possessive Pronouns

Possessive pronouns can take the place of possessive nouns.
Mine, yours, his, hers, its, ours, and theirs are possessive pronouns.

Circle the possessive pronoun in each sentence.

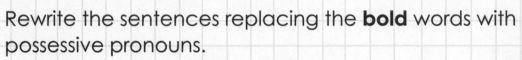

1 The blue car is (ours).

2 The rocket painting is mine.

3 Here is my bag, and there is hers.

4 Are these shoes yours?

5 Theirs is the next classroom.

Rewrite the sentences replacing the **bold** words with possessive pronouns.

1 That's your jacket, and this is **my jacket**.
   That's your jacket, and this is mine.

2 This is my seat, and that's **your seat**.
   _____

3 I think this car might be **their car**.
   _____

4 Your dog is a poodle, and **our dog** is a terrier.
   _____

5 Do you think this office is **her office**?
   _____

Match Antecedents

We often use pronouns and possessive adjectives to avoid repeating nouns. A word's **antecedent** is the noun that it refers back to.

Rewrite the sentences replacing the **bold** words with matching pronouns or possessive adjectives.

1 I saw Caleb riding **Caleb's** new bike.

I saw Caleb riding his new bike.

2 Dad jumped when I gave **Dad** a fright.

_____

3 Livvy ate pizza while **Livvy** watched TV.

_____

4 The Smiths are here. I invited **the Smiths** for dinner.

_____

5 The truck kept going until **the truck** reached the depot.

_____

Write the correct pronoun or possessive adjective to match the antecedent.

1 Ryan ran home with _his_ heart beating fast.

2 The astronauts put on _____ spacesuits.

3 Mom listened to the radio while _____ drove to work.

4 The female dinosaur laid _____ eggs in a soft nest.

5 After Ben and Nora finished their work, _____ went for a swim.

Adjectives

Adjectives are **describing words**. They describe nouns. Funny, orange, massive, hairy, and muddy are adjectives.

Circle each adjective and draw an arrow to the noun that it describes. There are two adjectives in each sentence.

1 The (hungry) dog stole (two) sausages.

2 Jaden wore his striped T-shirt with his orange shorts.

3 Why is that huge hippo making that loud noise?

4 I baked round cookies and rectangular brownies.

5 The chips are salty, and the fish is fresh.

6 The frog felt slimy, and the toad felt bumpy.

7 Today, the weather is cold and windy.

8 I've got five dollars and a few coins.

9 Look at that funny, fluffy rabbit!

Write four adjectives that describe your favorite food.

_____   _____   _____   _____

Main Verbs and Helping Verbs

Main verbs are doing words, or action words, such as *walk*, *think*, and *ask*. Helping verbs go in front of main verbs. They include *am*, *is*, *will*, *were*, *was*, *has*, *do*, *should*, *must*, and *can*.

Circle the main verb in **red** and the helping verb in **blue**.

1 Oliver (will) (run) in tomorrow's race.

2 Harper is visiting her best friend.

3 I was working hard.

4 Noah has finished his homework.

5 You must help Jamie.

6 She should ask Connor.

7 I can ride a skateboard.

8 We were thinking about you.

Write a sentence using the helping verb in parentheses and a main verb.

1 (will) _____

2 (can) _____

Adverbs

Adverbs are words that we add to a verb or adjective to tell us more about it. Many adverbs end in the letters -ly.

Write each adverb into the chart to show what sort of information it tells us. Then add one more word to each column.

~~today~~	~~here~~	~~easily~~	far	frequently	up	now	slowly
tomorrow	gently	always	carefully	everywhere	loudly
inside	wildly	safely	sometimes	enormously	nowhere
down	then	anywhere	yesterday	shyly	soon

How?	When?	Where?
easily	today	here

Write an adverb in each sentence.

1 Logan _____ opened his gift.

2 I _____ completed the puzzle.

3 I will do my chores _____ .

4 Chloe ran _____ to the finish line.

Tenses

We change verbs to show if the action in a sentence happened in the **past** (past tense), is happening **now** (present tense), or will happen in the **future** (future tense).

Write **past**, **present**, or **future** after each sentence to show which tense it is written in.

I will go for a swim this afternoon. _____

Layla ate her lunch with Mia. _____

Eli will be in fourth grade next year. _____

Evelyn likes art class best of all. _____

Jayden played football before dinner. _____

I can see a cloud that looks like a dog. _____

Write the correct form of the verb in each sentence.
You will need to use *will* and another verb for the future tense.

1 I _____ slowly home from school. (past tense of *walk*)

2 James __ _____ his cousin tomorrow. (future tense of *visit*)

3 Wyatt _____ this game every day. (present tense of *play*)

4 Eliana _____ her favorite movie last night. (past tense of *watch*)

5 Vicky _____ to greet her best friend. (present tense of *rush*)

6 I __ _____ my bike to your house. (future tense of *ride*)

Full Sentences

A full sentence must have two things: a **subject** and a **verb**.
Most sentences have other words as well.

For each sentence, underline the subject in **red** and the verb or verbs in **green**. Some sentences will have other words as well.

1 <u>The old house</u> is sweltering in the hot sun.

2 Isaac dances.

3 Hailey writes.

4 It sits on the shelf.

5 This cat sleeps all day.

6 My mother jumps on the trampoline.

7 Henry Jones is dreaming about soccer.

Put a **check** beside each full sentence. Put an **X** by the fragments that are not full sentences.

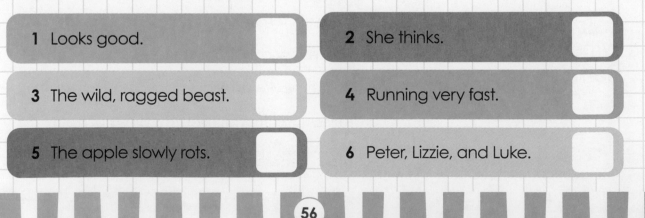

1 Looks good.

2 She thinks.

3 The wild, ragged beast.

4 Running very fast.

5 The apple slowly rots.

6 Peter, Lizzie, and Luke.

Types of Sentences

A **simple sentence** has one complete idea. A **compound sentence** has two complete ideas. A **complex sentence** has a complete idea and a dependent clause, which needs the first idea to make sense.

Write **simple** or **compound** to describe each sentence.

1 Maria loves reading, and Max likes playing guitar. _____

2 Here comes the principal. _____

3 I like pizza, but I don't like pepperoni. _____

4 Cora and Elias raced to the gate. _____

5 The wind blew, and then the hail fell. _____

6 It might snow soon. _____

Write **compound** or **complex** to describe each sentence.

1 Do you want some cake, or do you want ice cream? _____

2 When the sun comes out, we will go to the park. _____

3 The baby cried, and the toddler screamed. _____

4 I don't want a snack now, but I will soon. _____

5 If it turns cold, put on a jacket. _____

6 I fed the cat, and then I walked the dog. _____

Write a simple sentence, a compound sentence, and a complex sentence.

(simple) _____

(compound) _____

(complex) _____

Comparatives and Superlatives

> Most, but not all, **comparatives** end in **-er**. For example, *bigger, fluffier*.
> Most, but not all, **superlatives** end in **-est**. For example, *biggest, fluffiest*.

Complete the chart. If you're unsure of a word or its spelling, look up the adjective in a dictionary.

Adjective	Comparative	Superlative
long	longer	
		slowest
	larger	
		finest
	happier	
		busiest
	sadder	
		hottest
good	better	
bad		worst
popular	more popular	
		most interesting

Use your filled-in chart above to complete these spelling rules.

When a word ends in _____, just add -r or -st.

When an adjective ends in -y, change the y to an _____, before adding -er or -est.

For consonant-vowel-consonant (CVC) words, double the last _____, before adding -er or -est.

For words of three or more syllables, use *more* to make the comparative and use _____ to make the superlative.

Conjunctions

Coordinating conjunctions join equally important words, phrases, or complete ideas. Subordinating conjunctions join dependent clauses to the main clause.

Put a coordinating conjunction into each sentence.

and	but	or	so	yet	nor

1 Do you want to go skating, _____ do you want lunch?

2 I usually love swimming, _____ I don't feel like it today.

3 I love this blue top, _____ I also like this red one.

4 Audrey is good at math, _____ she might help you with it.

5 I've been working for hours, _____ I'm still not finished.

6 Kai never wanted a dog, _____ did he want a cat.

Put a subordinating conjunction into each sentence.

before	because	until	while	although	After

1 _____ you've made your bed, you're free to play.

2 I'm late _____ my alarm clock didn't go off.

3 Please stay inside _____ it stops raining.

4 My sister is a great friend, _____ she is annoying sometimes.

5 I like to draw pictures _____ I watch TV.

6 Elliot eats breakfast _____ he goes to school.

Commas in Sentences

Commas tell readers when to pause. Put a comma after a dependent clause or phrase that sits at the start of a sentence.

Add a comma after the dependent clause in each sentence.

1 If you start shouting, you'll wake Dad.

2 When you're ready you can join the game.

3 Before I met you I didn't know any famous people.

4 After we eat we should watch a movie.

5 While you're away I will call you every day.

Add a comma after the introductory word or phrase in each sentence.

1 With a brave smile, she stepped onto the stage.

2 Without thinking he rushed to the baby's rescue.

3 Last week my brother passed his driving test.

4 In 2012 my parents met at a party.

5 If there's room you can come with us.

Rewrite each sentence with a dependent clause or phrase at the start.

1 I saw a dolphin leap out of the water.

When we went to the beach, I saw a dolphin leap out of the water.

2 Put on sunscreen and a hat.

_____

3 The dog ate the meatloaf.

_____

Commas in Dialogue

Put a comma before the closing speech marks if there are more words in the sentence. Put a comma after words like said if they come before the spoken words.

Add speech marks and a comma to each sentence. Use the example sentence to see where to put capital letters.

1 Amelia said this is the best book I've ever read.

Amelia said, "This is the best book I've ever read."

2 Mom said let's go to the lake tomorrow.

_____

3 I'd love to work with computers Lily said.

_____

4 Mrs. Evans announced we are going to put on a play.

_____

5 I'd like to be a vet said Daniel.

_____

Rewrite each sentence changing the indirect speech to direct speech. Use the example sentence to see where to put commas.

1 Liam told Harry that his laces were undone.

"Harry, your laces are undone," Liam said.

2 Arianna said that she felt too tired to keep going.

_____

3 Josiah shouted at Maddie to watch out for the cars.

_____

Prefixes

A **prefix** is a group of letters we add to the start of a word to change its meaning. For example, the prefix mis- changes **behave** to **misbehave**.

Add a prefix to each word in **bold** to make its opposite.
You can use the same prefix more than once.

| in- | im- | dis- | un- | mis- |

1 not **visible** _____invisible_____   2 not to **trust** _____

3 not **comfortable** _____   4 not **honest** _____

5 not **secure** _____   6 to **spell** incorrectly _____

7 not **known** _____   8 not to **agree** _____

9 to **behave** badly _____   10 not **proper** _____

11 not **possible** _____   12 not **active** _____

Complete the chart using words you didn't use above.

Prefix	Definition	Prefix + Word	Word Definition
un-	not / change back	unhappy	not happy
un-	_____	un_____	_____
im-	_____	im_____	_____
dis-	_____	dis_____	_____
in-	_____	in_____	_____
mis-	_____	mis_____	_____

Prefixes

Add the prefixes to the words to create new words.

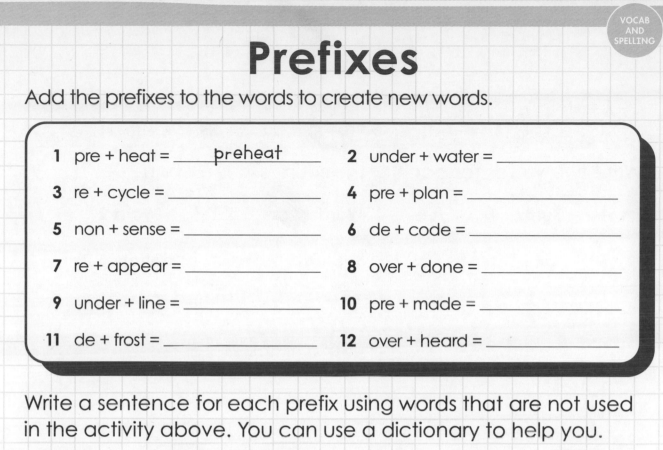

1 pre + heat = _preheat_

2 under + water = _____

3 re + cycle = _____

4 pre + plan = _____

5 non + sense = _____

6 de + code = _____

7 re + appear = _____

8 over + done = _____

9 under + line = _____

10 pre + made = _____

11 de + frost = _____

12 over + heard = _____

Write a sentence for each prefix using words that are not used in the activity above. You can use a dictionary to help you.

pre-   under-   over-   non-   de-   re-

1 _____

2 _____

3 _____

4 _____

5 _____

6 _____

Suffixes

A **suffix** is a group of letters we add to the end of a word to change its meaning. For example, the suffix **-ness** changes **dark** to **darkness**.

Write two words for each of the suffixes in the chart.

Suffix	Word 1	Word 2
-ful	hopeful	delightful
-ly		
-less		
-ness		
-ment		
-tion		

We add the suffix **-ed** to some verbs to change them into the **past tense**. Sometimes, if the verb ends in **-y**, we change it to i before adding **-ed**.

Rewrite each sentence, putting the word in parentheses into the past tense.

1 Eleanor (hurry) to catch the train.

Eleanor hurried to catch the train.

2 The crowd (cheer) when the star striker scored.

_____

3 Dad (visit) the store on his way home.

_____

4 Tommy (cry) when he fell over.

_____

Suffixes

The suffixes -er, -or, -ist, and -ian all mean **someone who**. For example, a **writer** is someone who writes, and an **editor** is someone who edits.

Read the text. Then add the correct suffix to each of the **bold** words. You may need to use a dictionary.

Showtime!

The day of the talent show arrived, and everyone was ready to perform. Aaron was first on stage. He started to **sing** like an angel, while Maria accompanied him on her **violin**.

Next, Levi astonished the audience with his **magic** act. Then Adam made everyone laugh until their sides hurt with his **comedy** sketch. Violet **juggled**, Hazel played the **piano**, Josh did a tap **dance**, and Penelope and Lila had a **rap** battle.

Finally, Nathan and Sadie closed the show. They chose to **act** out a scene from their favorite play. The event was a big success, and it ran smoothly because Mrs. Thomas was there to **direct** the whole show.

sing → _singer_   violin → _____

magic → _____   comedy → _____

juggled → _____   piano → _____

dance → _____   rap → _____

act → _____   direct → _____

Root Words

The part of a word that we add a prefix or a suffix to is called the **root word**. For example, **grace** is the root word of **graceful** and **disgrace**.

Fill in the boxes using words that stem from each root word.

like	**play**	**light**	**form**
likeness	played	lightly	inform

Complete the chart. You can use a dictionary to help you.

Word	Root Word	Root Word Definition
activity	active	busy or energetic
impolite		
powerful		
youngster		
incorrect		
lovely		
addition		

Compound Words

> We can join two words together to make a compound word with a new meaning. For example, some and thing make something.

Draw lines to make compound words. Then write the compound words in the box.

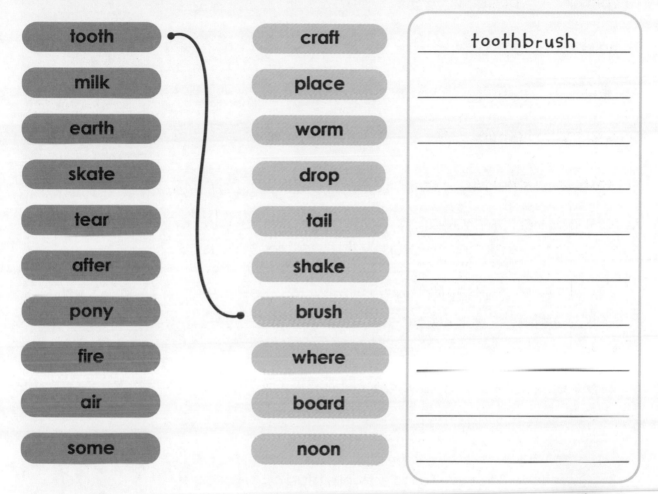

tooth	craft
milk	place
earth	worm
skate	drop
tear	tail
after	shake
pony	brush
fire	where
air	board
some	noon

toothbrush

Circle the compound word hidden on each row.

limestone	forgetful	deserving	between
thought	together	notebook	shorten
mountain	children	peanut	disconnect
problem	unstoppable	happened	downhill
several	handshake	important	example

Synonyms

A **synonym** is a word that has the same or a similar meaning to another word. For example, a synonym of **shy** is **timid**.

Write a synonym for each word to make a rhyming pair.

big	boat	⟶	__large__	__barge__
noisy	group	⟶		
tiny	tumble	⟶		
upset	father	⟶		
fast	choice	⟶		

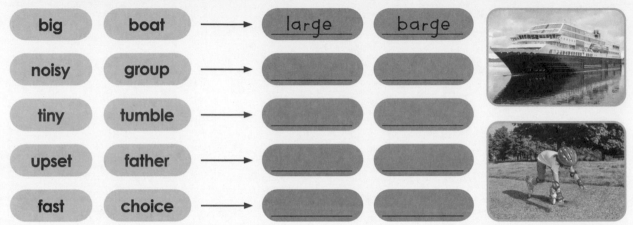

Circle the words that are synonyms. Then rewrite each sentence, swapping the circled words with another synonym.

1 My sister is a ⟨nice⟩ and ⟨loving⟩ person.
   <u>My sister is a kind person.</u>

2 Mateo shouted and screamed when he banged his leg.
   _____

3 Owen chuckled and giggled while reading his book.
   _____

4 Charlotte bought gorgeous dresses and pretty shoes.
   _____

5 Avery was sleepy and drowsy after a long day at the park.
   _____

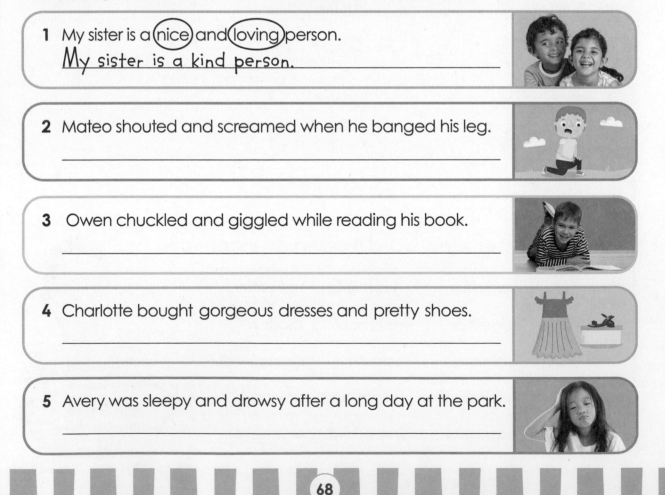

Antonyms

An **antonym** is a word that has the opposite meaning to another word.
For example, an antonym of **exciting** is **boring**.

Shade the flags **blue** if the word pairs are synonyms.
Shade the flags **orange** if the word pairs are antonyms.

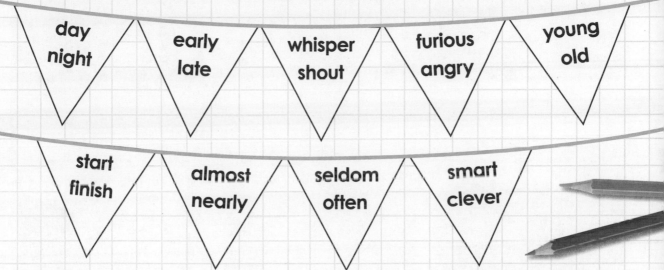

| day night | early late | whisper shout | furious angry | young old |

| start finish | almost nearly | seldom often | smart clever |

Rewrite the sentences using an antonym of each **bold** word.

1 Today, it will be **warm** outside.
Today, it will be cold outside.

2 Xander's cup was **empty**.

_____

3 Anna couldn't stop **laughing** at the movie.

_____

4 Ezra always **forgets** his friends' birthdays.

_____

5 Savannah is the **shortest** girl in the class.

_____

Homophones

A **homophone** is a word that sounds like another word but has a different spelling and meaning. For example, a homophone of **piece** is **peace**.

Write the two homophones shown by each picture clue.

rain

rein

Fill in the blanks with homophones from the word bank.

bear	~~grown~~	heard	plane	road
rode	~~groan~~	bare	herd	plain

1 Layla let out a __groan__ because her flowers hadn't __grown__.

2 The _____ flew over the dusty _____ .

3 The _____ of antelope _____ the lion coming.

4 Sam _____ his horse down the long _____ .

5 The grizzly _____ slept under a tree that was _____ of leaves.

Homographs

A **homograph** is a word with the same spelling as another word but a different meaning. It sometimes sounds different as well.

Read the clues. Then write the homograph in the middle box.

the front of a ship	bow	a hair ribbon
the outer layer of a tree trunk		the sound a dog makes
an area of public land		to bring a vehicle to a stop
a stone		a type of music
a leader of a country		a tool used to measure length

Circle the homographs in each sentence, and then write the two definitions. You can use a dictionary to help you.

Ethan turned right because he was sure it was the right way.

1 _____

2 _____

Did the store close to our house close?

1 _____

2 _____

Grandma rose from her chair to water her rose.

1 _____

2 _____

Elijah pressed his palm against the rough trunk of the palm tree.

1 _____

2 _____

Double Consonants

Words with a **double consonant** spelling pattern have a consonant that is repeated next to itself.

Complete the words by adding the correct double consonants. Then write more words that contain double consonants.

| bb | gg | rr | ss | tt | nn | ff | dd | mm |

gi _gg_ le   li ___ le   bu ___ le

che ___ y   ri ___ on   co ___ ect

bo ___ le   ki ___ en   di ___ erent

su ___ er   fu ___ y   pu ___ le

ma ___ er   le ___ on   emba ___ a ___

_____   _____   _____

If a one-syllable word ends in a short vowel and a consonant, we **double the consonant** before adding **-ed** or **-ing**. Words ending in **-x** don't obey this rule.

Complete the chart. Then circle the double consonants.

Word	Add -ed.	Add -ing.
stop	sto(pp)ed	sto(pp)ing
grin		
box		
pop		
mix		
relax		
blur		

Consonant Digraphs

A **consonant digraph** is two consonants that are written together to spell one sound. They include: **sh, ch, th, wh, ph,** and **ng.**

Sort the stickers into the correct groups.

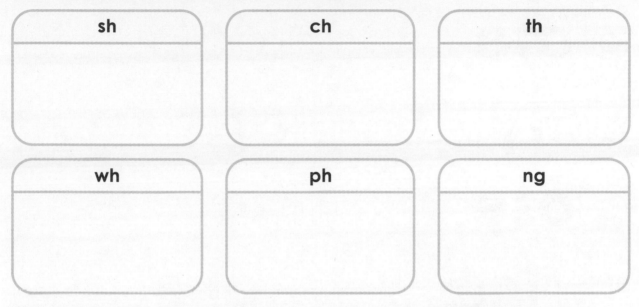

sh	ch	th

wh	ph	ng

Complete the chart. You can use a dictionary to help you.

Unscramble it.	Write it.	Define it.
shdea __shade__	shade	A patch of darkness where light does not reach.
ewch _____		
waht _____		
ootht _____		
nyuog _____		
thlhae _____		

Consonant Clusters

A **consonant cluster** is two or more consonants that appear together in a word. When we read clusters aloud, we hear each consonant sound.

Shade the consonant clusters. Then cover and write the words.

plate _____   **group** _____

story _____   **flag** _____

close _____   **tree** _____

spring _____   **snake** _____

Write as many words as you can in the boxes by adding different consonant clusters to these endings.

-ay	-ow	-ain
stay		

Silent Letters

A **silent letter** is a letter that becomes silent when combined with other letters. For example, **climb** is spelled with a silent **b**.

Circle the silent letters in these silly sentences.

1 The (h)onest ca(l)f clim(b)ed the hill.

2 Isla gnawed on the knob of butter.

3 The knight guarded the guilty ghost.

4 Who wrote the rhyming answer?

5 A lamb sang hymns for an hour.

6 I sailed my yacht to a gnome's island.

Write silly sentences using these or other words with silent letters.

doubt	crumb	science	Wednesday	sign	could	talk
when	listen	walk	know	knit	knock	honor	where
what	whale	castle	ballet	wrong	two	kneel	whole

1 _____

2 _____

3 _____

4 _____

5 _____

6 _____

Vowel + r Sounds

Vowel sounds often change when they are followed by the letter r. For example, the e in **her** sounds different to the e in **hen** and **hem**.

Read each word aloud and listen to the vowel sound.
Then use the key to shade each rectangle the correct color.

ar = yellow   **er** = blue   **ir** = red   **or** = green   **ur** = purple

star	curl	first	car	her	girl
turn	sport	market	serve	morning	hurt
pork	twirl	nurse	germ	hard	fork
chart	person	farm	circle	turtle	storm

Sort the words from the activity above into the correct columns in the chart.

-ar	-er	-or	-ir	-ur
star				

Multisyllabic Words

Unscramble the syllables in each word. Then circle the 2-syllable words in **red**, the 3-syllable words in **green**, the 4-syllable words in **blue**, and the 5-syllable words in **pink**.

1 (on / ter / wa / mel) watermelon   2 e / el / phant _____

3 Sat / day / ur _____   4 tween / be _____

5 por / im / tant _____   6 li / cop / he / ter _____

7 wich / sand _____   8 mul / ca / ti / tion / pli _____

9 cit / ex / ing _____   10 cat / er / lar / pil _____

11 ing / pen / hap _____   12 tions / grat / u / la / con _____

Fill in the blanks with words that have the number of syllables shown in the parentheses.

1 Mom reads the (3) _____ every morning.

2 The teacher demonstrated the science (4) _____ to the class.

3 Carl was excited for his birthday in (3) _____ .

4 (3) _____ are one of the first flowers of spring.

5 Lily baked (2) _____ after school.

6 David wrote a story about a (4) _____ who saved the world.

7 Josh went to the zoo and saw (2) _____ and (4) _____ .

8 Mackenzie wrote the words in (5) _____ order.

Shades of Meaning

Shades of meaning are the small differences between synonyms. Happy and ecstatic are both positive emotions, but ecstatic is a stronger feeling.

Circle the word that doesn't belong in each group.

happy   satisfied   ecstatic   worried   delighted

fatigued   tired   cold   sleepy   exhausted

adore   hate   love   like   admire

angry   clever   smart   genius   brilliant

knew   believed   suspected   helped   thought

Put the words in each box in order from weakest to strongest.

enormous   huge   big

1 ___big___   2 ___huge___   3 ___enormous___

good   perfect   great

1 _____   2 _____   3 _____

irritated   furious   angry

1 _____   2 _____   3 _____

ran   jogged   sprinted

1 _____   2 _____   3 _____

worried   terrified   scared

1 _____   2 _____   3 _____

Context Clues

Context clues are clues to a word's meaning in nearby text and pictures.

Use the sentences to figure out and write the definitions of the words in **bold**.

1 The small **tributary** branched off the wide Mississippi River.

_____

2 The sweet **aroma** of the dessert drifted from the kitchen.

_____

3 Jessica's teeth chattered as she stood in the **frigid** air.

_____

4 Eve balanced **precariously** on the narrow gymnastics beam.

_____

5 The whispered conversation wasn't **audible** to the crowd outside.

_____

6 Josiah had a **plethora** of excuses for his lateness, but his friends didn't believe him because none of them were **credible**.

_____

_____

7 Theo couldn't follow the long, **convoluted** instructions, so he asked the teacher to **clarify** them.

_____

_____

Know and Learn

Before you start **researching**, write notes on what you know about a topic and what you'd like to know. After researching, add what you learned.

Write what you know and what you would like to know about alligators. Use books, an encyclopedia, or the Internet to learn more. Then write what you learned.

Alligators

I Know	I Want to Know	I Learned
• Alligators have tails covered in thick, tough scales.	• A main difference between alligators and crocodiles.	• Alligators have U-shaped faces and crocodiles have V-shaped.
• _____	• _____	• _____
• _____	• _____	• _____

Pick a different animal and complete the chart. Write three things in each column.

Animal: _____

I Know	I Want to Know	I Learned
• _____	• _____	• _____
• _____	• _____	• _____
• _____	• _____	• _____

Take Notes

Taking notes helps you remember important details. Notes do not have to be full sentences and should not be copied word for word from the source.

Use books, an encyclopedia, or the Internet to learn more about each country. Write four interesting details about each one.

Guatemala

- country in Central America, south of Mexico
- capital is Guatemala City
- Spanish is official language
- population over 16 million

Brazil

- _____
- _____
- _____
- _____

Mexico

- _____
- _____
- _____
- _____

Argentina

- _____
- _____
- _____
- _____

Map Libraries

Libraries are usually divided into different sections, such as **fiction** and **nonfiction**.

Draw lines to match the book titles to the correct category.

Some libraries divide books into categories, or genres, such as science fiction or geography. Visit a library and find one title for each genre. Write the name of each book and its author.

plays	science fiction	geography	animals	biographies
Romeo and Juliet by William Shakespeare				

Table of Contents

A **table of contents** is a list at the beginning of a book that tells you the name of each chapter and its page number.

Use the table of contents to answer the questions.

1 What is the name of chapter 5?

_____

2 On what page does chapter 7 start? _____

3 Which famous volcanoes have their own chapter?

_____

_____

4 If you want to learn how eruptions occur, which chapter should you read?

_____

Index

An **index** is a list at the end of a book that tells you on what pages you can find specific topics. Usually, only nonfiction books have an index.

Use this portion of an index to answer the questions.

Fossils

A
Ammonites 21–22
Amphibians 14, 29
Arthropods 32, 54–55

B
Birds 15–16, 30
Brachiosaurus 7, 13 (*see also* Dinosaurs)

C
Claosaurus 10 (*see also* Dinosaurs)
Cretaceous Period 58

D
Dinosaurs 7, 10, 13, 28
Dudley bug 35

1 On what pages can you find information about birds?

_____

2 On what pages can you find information about amphibians?

_____

3 What information might you find on page 58?

_____

4 Based on the index, which two dinosaurs do you know are included in this book?

_____

Find a nonfiction book with an index. Use the index to look up a topic that interests you. Write a new fact you've learned about the topic here.

_____

_____

Dictionary Practice

We use a **dictionary** to find the meaning and spelling of a word.
Dictionaries list words in alphabetical order.

Read the text from *A Little Princess* by Frances Hodgson Burnett. Circle four new or difficult words. Use a dictionary to find their meanings. Then use each word in a sentence.

Never did she find anything so difficult as to keep herself from losing her temper when she was suddenly disturbed while absorbed in a book. People who are fond of books know the feeling of irritation which sweeps over them at such a moment. The temptation to be unreasonable and snappish is one not easy to manage.

Word	Meaning	Sentence

Glossary

A **glossary** is a list of important or difficult words used in a book.

Help create a glossary. Match each word with its meaning.
Then rewrite the words with their meanings in alphabetical order.

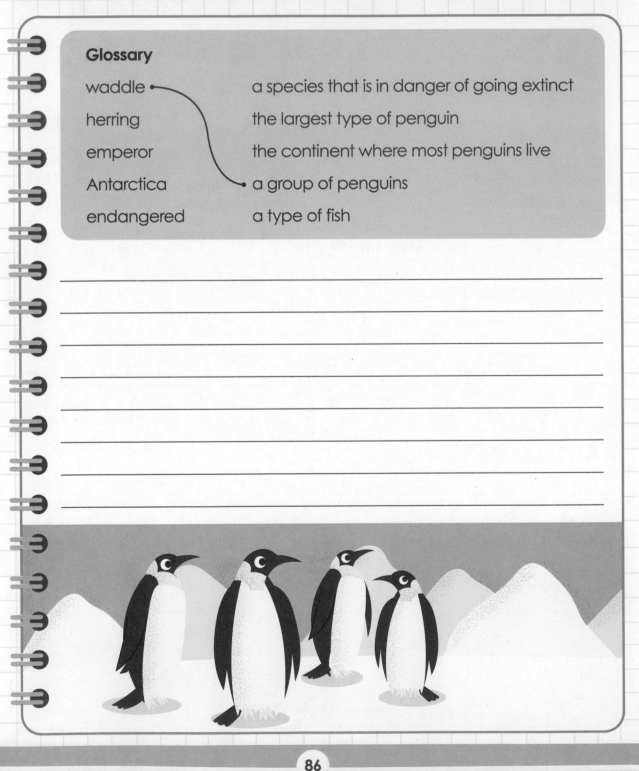

Glossary

waddle	a species that is in danger of going extinct
herring	the largest type of penguin
emperor	the continent where most penguins live
Antarctica	a group of penguins
endangered	a type of fish

Internet Safety

The Internet is a great tool for research and communication, but you need to stay safe online.

Sticker the correct word into each safety instruction.

1 Ask a _____ before contacting a stranger online.

2 Do not _____ on ads.

3 If a warning message appears, tell an _____.

4 Create a _____ to protect your information.

5 Don't share _____ information, such as your address, online.

6 Never _____ something online without asking permission first.

Cover the answers above, and write three safety rules for using the Internet.

1 _____

2 _____

3 _____

Passwords should be easy for you to remember but difficult for others to guess. Circle good passwords in **green**. Put a **red X** over bad passwords that are easy for your friends to guess.

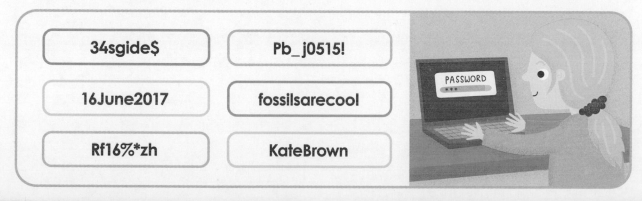

34sgide$

Pb_j0515!

16June2017

fossilsarecool

Rf16%*zh

KateBrown

Online Resources

Web addresses ending in **.org** or **.gov** often have reliable, fact-checked information. Those ending in **.com** or **.net** can be created by anybody, so be careful!

Circle the best websites for researching George Washington in **green**, and ones that might be reliable in **yellow**. Put a **red X** over websites that you shouldn't use (especially if they have a spelling mistake).

georgewashington.com	ilovegeorgewashington.net
uspresidents.gov	goergewashignton.com
presidentwashington.net	thewashingtonproject.org

Read the two texts below. Underline facts that are the same in **blue**, and underline facts that are different or unique in **orange**.

Source 1:
As a toddler, Helen Keller became sick and lost her eyesight and hearing. A young teacher called Anne Sullivan helped Helen learn to read and write. The two remained friends for life.

Source 2:
Helen Keller could not speak or hear. Anne Sullivan, who had been blind but regained her eyesight through surgery, is known as the "miracle worker" because she taught Helen to read and write. Helen became an author.

Use the Internet to find a reliable source to check one fact you underlined in blue and one fact you underlined in orange. Were they accurate?

Search Engines

Search engines pull together information from the Internet. Sometimes companies pay money to have their websites appear at the top of search results.

Read the two texts. Write which text you think is informational and which is an ad.

The number of polar bears in the world is decreasing, and their Arctic habitat is under threat. By sending $3 a month, you can help to save the polar bears.

_____

Polar bears are marine animals. They live in the Arctic and hunt in the icy sea. As the ice caps melt, polar bears are spending more time hunting on land, and their diet is changing.

_____

You'll get the best search engine results if you only include the most important words, or **keywords**.
Underline the keywords below.

On which <u>continents</u> do <u>polar</u> <u>bears</u> <u>live</u>? 🔍

What do penguins eat? 🔍

What is the largest ocean in the world? 🔍

What different types of seals are there? 🔍

To what age do dolphins usually live? 🔍

News or Point of View?

News sources publish **factual news reports** as well as **points of view,** which are opinions.

Write which headlines are news, and which are points of view.

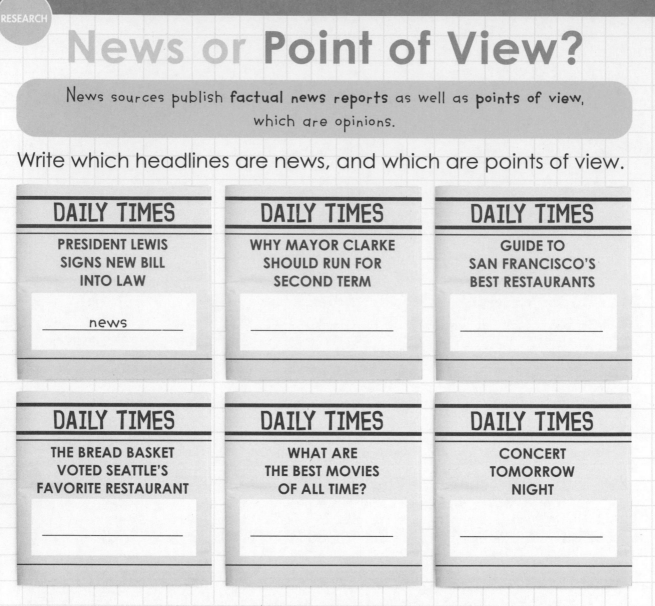

DAILY TIMES

PRESIDENT LEWIS
SIGNS NEW BILL
INTO LAW

news

DAILY TIMES

WHY MAYOR CLARKE
SHOULD RUN FOR
SECOND TERM

_____

DAILY TIMES

GUIDE TO
SAN FRANCISCO'S
BEST RESTAURANTS

_____

DAILY TIMES

THE BREAD BASKET
VOTED SEATTLE'S
FAVORITE RESTAURANT

_____

DAILY TIMES

WHAT ARE
THE BEST MOVIES
OF ALL TIME?

_____

DAILY TIMES

CONCERT
TOMORROW
NIGHT

_____

Some articles include facts and opinions. Read the text.
Underline facts in **green** and opinions in **red**.

Blizzard Memories

The Blizzard of 1996 hit on January 6 and lasted
for two days. It snowed 30 inches in Philadelphia,
and many roads closed. The temperature
dropped below 0° Fahrenheit. I was 8 years old,
and it was the coldest winter I can remember. We
had three days off school because of the snow,
and I built a snowman with my friends.
It was a magical time!

Blizzard of 1996

Presentations

When you **present**, you share your research with an audience. You can improve a presentation by writing key points on note cards and practicing it a few times.

Research a famous person and plan a presentation about them. Write down what you'd like to say in your speech.

Here are a few things to include:

- the person's full name
- when they were born
- where they live
- what they're famous for.

First, introduce the person you chose.

_____
_____
_____
_____
_____

Next, explain why you picked this person.

_____
_____
_____
_____
_____

Write the three most important things you want your audience to learn.

- _____
  _____
- _____
  _____
- _____
  _____

Conclude by telling your audience why they should learn more about this person.

_____
_____
_____
_____
_____

Create a Survey

A **survey** is a research method where an interviewer asks people for their opinions on a topic.

Ask at least six friends the following question. Tally their answers.

Which of these sports do you like best?	Number of Answers
football	_____
hockey	_____
tennis	_____
swimming	_____

Which sport was the most popular answer? _____

Which was the least popular? _____

Think of a question to ask at least six friends. Write the question and four options. Then tally your friends' answers.

Question _____	Number of Answers
option 1 _____	_____
option 2 _____	_____
option 3 _____	_____
option 4 _____	_____

Which answer was the most popular? _____

Which was the least popular? _____

Did any results surprise you? Why? _____

_____

Brainstorming

When planning a project, first **brainstorm** a list of topics you would like to research.

Brainstorm two countries you'd like to visit. Write the name of the country, what you know about the country, and what you'd like to learn.

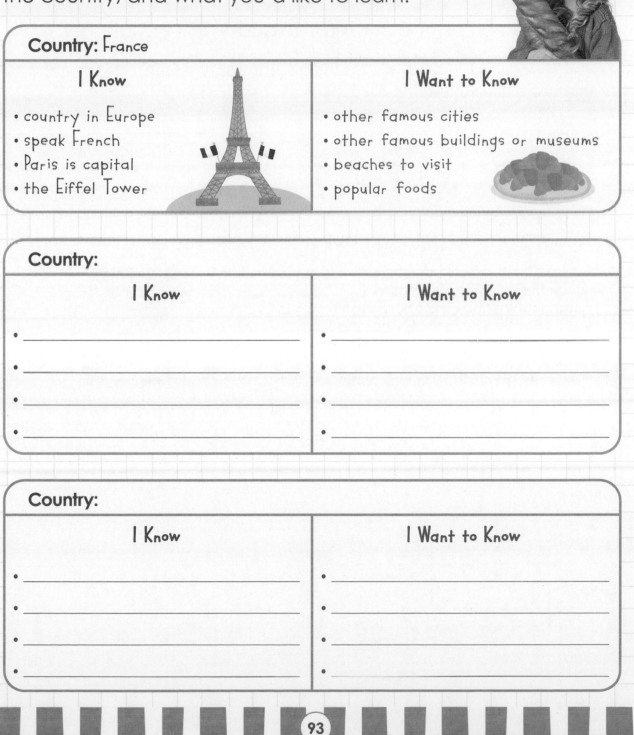

Country: France

I Know	I Want to Know
• country in Europe	• other famous cities
• speak French	• other famous buildings or museums
• Paris is capital	• beaches to visit
• the Eiffel Tower	• popular foods

Country:

I Know	I Want to Know
• _____	• _____
• _____	• _____
• _____	• _____
• _____	• _____

Country:

I Know	I Want to Know
• _____	• _____
• _____	• _____
• _____	• _____
• _____	• _____

Plan Your Research

Creating a plan helps you to **identify your research goals** and reason for writing. It helps save time.

Pick one country from page 93 to research.

Country: _____

List some resources. You can include books and the Internet. Write specific book titles or web addresses, if you can.

- <u>A History of France (book)</u>
- _____
- _____
- _____

Write notes in the box. Use bullet points or a mind map.

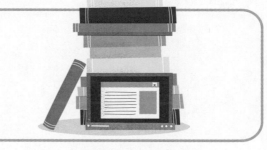

Include the following information:
- the country's name and continent
- the country's capital city and languages
- three cities or landmarks you'd like to see
- the sorts of foods people eat
- why people should visit this country.

Plan Your Report

Writers plan before they write. Some create **outlines**.

Create an outline for your report.

First, introduce the topic of your report.

Introduction: I'd like to visit France.

Next, think about what facts you want to include.

Supporting details:
- country in Europe
- food: cheese, escargots, bouillabaisse
- popular cities: Paris, Nice, Marseille, Lille
- things I want to see: the Eiffel Tower, the Louvre, Mont-Saint-Michel

Finally, finish your report with a sentence that brings the information together.

Conclusion: People should visit France because it has delicious food and many interesting cities to see.

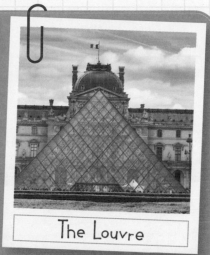

The Louvre

- Title: _____
- Introduction: _____
- _____
- Supporting details:
  - • _____
  - • _____
  - • _____
  - • _____
- Conclusion: _____
- _____

Draft a Report

For important pieces of text, writers often make a **rough draft** first.

Write the first draft of your report. Introduce the topic, and then add some interesting facts. Sum it up with a closing sentence.

_____

_____

_____

_____

_____

_____

_____

_____

_____

_____

_____

_____

_____

_____

Follow the steps below to edit your draft.

1 Circle any spellings you need to check in a dictionary.
2 Make sure you have used capital letters, commas, periods, and question marks in the right places.
3 Make sure your sentences make sense.
4 Decide what parts you want to change or improve.

Write a Report

Writers create a **final version** of a text using their draft and making changes to improve it.

Write or attach the final version of your report here.

Title: _____

_____

_____

_____

_____

_____

_____

_____

_____

_____

_____

_____

_____

_____

_____

_____

_____

_____

_____

_____

_____

_____

Draw a picture to go with
your report.

Place Value to 10,000

When writing numbers in standard form, don't forget to use 0 as a **placeholder** for any missing hundreds, tens, or ones.

Write the expanded-form numbers in standard form.

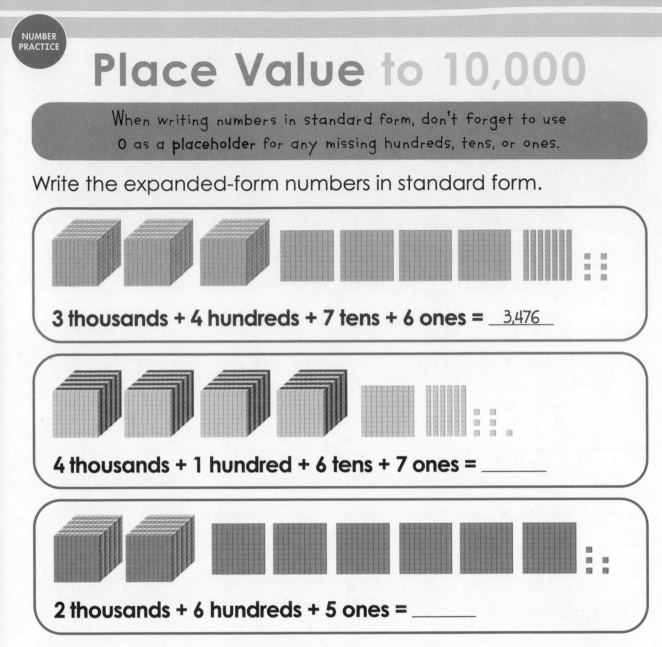

3 thousands + 4 hundreds + 7 tens + 6 ones = ___3,476___

4 thousands + 1 hundred + 6 tens + 7 ones = _____

2 thousands + 6 hundreds + 5 ones = _____

Write the digits that make up each number under the correct column in the place-value chart.

	thousands	hundreds	tens	ones
5,823	5	8	2	3
8,293				
2,737				
5,026				
8,520				
9,302				
900				

Standard Form

Remember that a **1** in any place-value column equals **10** of the column to its right. For example, 1,000 is ten 100s, and 100 is ten 10s.

Circle the value of each underlined digit.

5,2<u>9</u>6	9,000	900	90	9
<u>8</u>,362	8,000	800	80	8
6,28<u>7</u>	7,000	700	70	7
3,<u>4</u>71	4,000	400	40	4

Sticker the standard form of each expanded-form number.

8,000 + 600 + 90 + 4 =

2,000 + 800 + 50 + 9 =

6,000 + 200 + 60 + 6 =

3,000 + 900 + 2 =

2,000 + 400 + 60 =

4,000 + 50 + 2 =

Write the numbers in standard form.

nine-thousand, seven-hundred, thirty-five _____

five-thousand, four-hundred, eight _____

seven-thousand, six-hundred, thirteen _____

nine-thousand, nine-hundred, ninety _____

Four-thousand, three-hundred, fifty-two

=

4,352

Expanded Form

When expanding a number, say the number in **words** in your head.

Write the standard-form numbers as words.

8,240 eight-thousand, two-hundred, forty _____

2,694 _____

4,628 _____

6,802 _____

3,055 _____

7,520 _____

2,003 _____

Write the standard-form numbers in expanded form.

4,682 4,000 + 600 + 80 + 2 _____

5,791 _____

2,647 _____

8,206 _____

7,730 _____

4,018 _____

6,002 _____

9,999 _____

1,234 _____

6,300 _____

Number Comparisons

To find the larger number of two, compare the **highest value digits** first. For example, 611 is greater than 599 because 600 is higher than any 500 number.

Write < or > in each box.

8,235 ☐ 836   2,380 ☐ 2,379   7,023 ☐ 7,203

3,000 ☐ 2,999   5,283 ☐ 5,292   10,000 ☐ 9,999

2,350 ☐ 2,305   2,500 ☐ 2,055   7,001 ☐ 7,010

Write the numbers in order from smallest to largest.

6,346   6,340   6,400   5,999   5,349

_____

10,000   9,999   9,000   9,028   9,208

_____

1,000   1,010   1,100   1,110   999

_____

5,555   5,505   5,005   5,999   5,564

_____

4,628   2,034   1,923   6,203   7,234

_____

10,000   237   1,101   28   6,000

_____

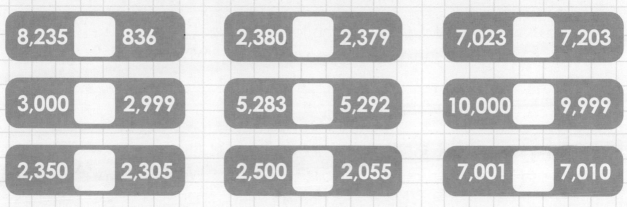

Word Problems

Word problems help us prepare for the ways we most often use math in **real life**.

Solve the word problems.

Amy has saved $789 dollars. She wants to buy a bike that costs $800. Does she have enough money yet? Why?

_____

A parking lot has room for 5,010 cars. Today, 4,011 drivers plan to use the parking lot. Will they all find a space? Why?

_____

A store owner buys 3,000 bananas, 20 pineapples, and 500 apples. How many pieces of fruit did she buy altogether?

_____

Mark's teacher asked him to write five-thousand, sixty on the board. Show the standard-form number that he wrote.

_____

What four-digit number has five thousands, no hundreds, no tens, and seven ones?

_____

Tom has saved $1,000. He takes it out of the bank in $100 bills. How many $100 bills will the bank teller give him?

_____

Round to a Ten

If the **ones digit** is **5** or higher, round up.
If the **ones digit** is **4** or lower, round down.

Round each **bold** number to the nearest 10 by circling the correct number.

(10)	**12**	20		30	**38**	40
10	**19**	20		90	**92**	100
40	**45**	50		70	**74**	80
80	**83**	90		20	**22**	30
50	**54**	60		90	**99**	100

Round each number to the nearest 10.

67 ☐	15 ☐	87 ☐	94 ☐	11 ☐
25 ☐	88 ☐	32 ☐	79 ☐	75 ☐

Solve the word problem.

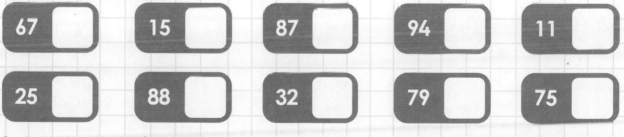

Grandpa said he'd pay Jack $1 for every minute he helped haul logs, and that he'd round the pay to the nearest $10. Jack hauled logs for 25 minutes. How much did Grandpa pay him?

$ _____

Round to a Hundred

If the **tens digit is 5** or higher, round up.
If the **tens digit is 4** or lower, round down.

Round each **bold** number to the nearest 100 by circling the correct number.

700	**782**	(800)	100	**115**	200
300	**347**	400	900	**994**	1,000
400	**483**	500	500	**545**	600
800	**825**	900	100	**160**	200
200	**229**	300	400	**449**	500

Round each number to the nearest 100.

384		101		278		919		294	
852		620		728		465		538	

Solve the word problem.

When selling her paintings, Ella figures out a price and then rounds it to the nearest hundred. Her latest painting came to a selling price of $614. How much did she put on the price tag?

$ ___

Place-Value Partitioning

Understanding place-value partitioning will help you understand column addition.

Break the numbers into tens and ones to help solve the problems.

46 + 72 = (40 + 70) + (6 + 2) = **110** + **8** = **118**
            tens   ones

74 + 12 = (70 + 10) + (4 + 2) = ☐ + ☐ = ☐
            tens   ones

62 + 33 = (☐ + ☐) + (☐ + ☐) = ☐ + ☐ = ☐
            tens   ones

54 + 85 = (☐ + ☐) + (☐ + ☐) = ☐ + ☐ = ☐
            tens   ones

26 + 92 = (☐ + ☐) + (☐ + ☐) = ☐ + ☐ = ☐
            tens   ones

73 + 55 = (☐ + ☐) + (☐ + ☐) = ☐ + ☐ = ☐
            tens   ones

56 + 64 = (☐ + ☐) + (☐ + ☐) = ☐ + ☐ = ☐
            tens   ones

37 + 25 = (☐ + ☐) + (☐ + ☐) = ☐ + ☐ = ☐
            tens   ones

46 + 27 = (☐ + ☐) + (☐ + ☐) = ☐ + ☐ = ☐
            tens   ones

Place-Value Partitioning

Place-value partitioning reminds you that each digit in a number has a different value depending on its position within the number.

Break the numbers into hundreds, tens, and ones to help solve the problems.

632 + 721 = (600 + 700) + (30 + 20) + (2+1) = 1,300 + 50 + 3 = 1,353

341 + 443 = (300 + 400) + (40 + 40) + (1+3) = ☐ + ☐ + ☐ = ☐

724 + 135 = (700 + 100) + (☐ + ☐) + (☐ + ☐) = ☐ + ☐ + ☐ = ☐

356 + 417 = (300 + 400) + (☐ + ☐) + (☐ + ☐) = ☐ + ☐ + ☐ = ☐

624 + 731 = (600 + 700) + (☐ + ☐) + (☐ + ☐) = ☐ + ☐ + ☐ = ☐

855 + 423 = (800 + 400) + (☐ + ☐) + (☐ + ☐) = ☐ + ☐ + ☐ = ☐

465 + 328 = (400 + 300) + (☐ + ☐) + (☐ + ☐) = ☐ + ☐ + ☐ = ☐

282 + 543 = (200 + 500) + (☐ + ☐) + (☐ + ☐) = ☐ + ☐ + ☐ = ☐

723 + 194 = (700 + 100) + (☐ + ☐) + (☐ + ☐) = ☐ + ☐ + ☐ = ☐

Column Addition

Solve the problems.

	10s	1s
	6	1
+	2	2
	8	3

	10s	1s
	5	5
+	3	4

	10s	1s
	7	7
+	2	2

61 + 22 = 83

55 + 34 =

77 + 22 =

	100s	10s	1s
	4	2	3
+	5	6	3

	100s	10s	1s
	7	3	1
+	2	4	8

423 + 563 =

731 + 248 =

Imagine the place-value columns above the numbers as you solve these problems.

```
   62        55        84
+  35     +  42     +  14
```

```
  734       623       252
+ 245     + 155     + 624
```

Add with Regrouping

Read the speech bubbles. They show you how to do addition when the sum of a column is greater than 9.

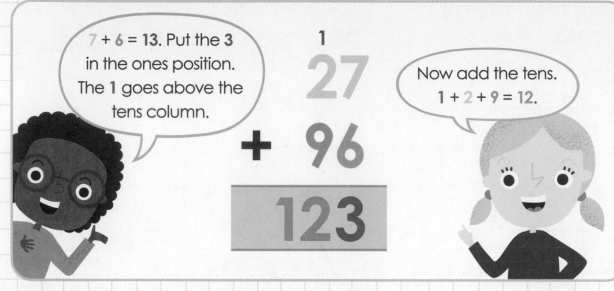

7 + 6 = 13. Put the **3** in the ones position. The **1** goes above the tens column.

1
27
+ 96
123

Now add the tens. 1 + 2 + 9 = 12.

Solve the problems using regrouping.

$$
\begin{array}{r} 1 \\ 35 \\ + 87 \\ \hline 122 \end{array}
\qquad
\begin{array}{r} 66 \\ + 76 \\ \hline \end{array}
\qquad
\begin{array}{r} 25 \\ + 48 \\ \hline \end{array}
\qquad
\begin{array}{r} 56 \\ + 49 \\ \hline \end{array}
$$

$$
\begin{array}{r} 72 \\ + 39 \\ \hline \end{array}
\qquad
\begin{array}{r} 17 \\ + 18 \\ \hline \end{array}
\qquad
\begin{array}{r} 55 \\ + 96 \\ \hline \end{array}
\qquad
\begin{array}{r} 21 \\ + 99 \\ \hline \end{array}
$$

Write an equation to solve the problem.

Riverton has 68 third graders at one school and 87 at another. How many third graders attend school in Riverton altogether?

Three-Digit Addition

When adding 3-digit numbers, you may need to carry a digit over to both the tens column and the hundreds column.

Solve the three-digit addition problems using regrouping.

```
  11
  758        642        517        337
+ 687      + 239      + 825      + 427
```
| 1,445 | | | |

```
  537        738        396        726
+ 657      + 676      + 284      + 823
```

```
  893        279        623        628
+ 467      + 899      + 907      + 267
```

Write equations to solve the word problems.

On Saturday, 157 people visited Sue's Shoe Store, and on Sunday, another 208 people visited. How many people visited over the whole weekend?

Hannah raised $127 to help refugees, and Luke raised $244. How much did they raise altogether?

Three-Digit Subtraction

When subtracting 3-digit numbers, you may need to borrow a hundred from the hundreds column in the same way as you borrow a ten from the tens column.

Solve the three-digit subtraction problems using regrouping.

5 16 13
$$\begin{array}{r} \not{6}73 \\ -\ 285 \\ \hline 388 \end{array}$$

$$\begin{array}{r} 585 \\ -\ 336 \\ \hline \end{array}$$

$$\begin{array}{r} 652 \\ -\ 427 \\ \hline \end{array}$$

$$\begin{array}{r} 984 \\ -\ 536 \\ \hline \end{array}$$

$$\begin{array}{r} 746 \\ -\ 539 \\ \hline \end{array}$$

$$\begin{array}{r} 592 \\ -\ 365 \\ \hline \end{array}$$

$$\begin{array}{r} 727 \\ -\ 638 \\ \hline \end{array}$$

$$\begin{array}{r} 463 \\ -\ 292 \\ \hline \end{array}$$

$$\begin{array}{r} 825 \\ -\ 655 \\ \hline \end{array}$$

$$\begin{array}{r} 991 \\ -\ 119 \\ \hline \end{array}$$

$$\begin{array}{r} 573 \\ -\ 566 \\ \hline \end{array}$$

$$\begin{array}{r} 682 \\ -\ 575 \\ \hline \end{array}$$

Write equations to solve the word problems.

452 people entered a singing contest. 384 were knocked out after the first round. How many made it to the next round?

686 children took beginners' art classes. The next year, 479 went on to the advanced classes. How many children stopped taking art classes after the first year?

Word Problems

With these word problems, first decide if you need to use **addition** or **subtraction** to solve the problem.

Write equations to solve the word problems.

Owen wants to buy a guinea-pig hutch for $56. So far, he has saved $38. How much more does he need to save?

On Friday, 543 people caught the first ferry to Sun Island. Another 467 people caught the second (and last) ferry. How many people traveled to the island that day?

On Saturday, Mila picked 25 plums from the tree in her yard.
On Sunday, she picked 47.
How many plums did she pick over the whole weekend?

Hailey scored 745 in her first game of Tower Maker, and 823 in her second game. What is the difference between her first and second scores?

Mr. Black wants to buy a jacket for $99 and a T-shirt for $45. Show a problem he could solve in his head to figure out the price of both items.

_____

Round and Add

Estimation is easier than complex addition. You can use it in a store to get a **rough idea** of how much you'll pay.

Estimate the sum by rounding to the nearest 10 or 100. Then solve the problems and compare the answer with the estimation. How close are they?

problem	estimation	problem	estimation
$\begin{array}{r} 1 \\ 49 \\ +\ 45 \\ \hline \end{array}$	$\begin{array}{r} \underline{50} \\ +\ 45 \\ \hline \end{array}$	$\begin{array}{r} 31 \\ +\ 54 \\ \hline \end{array}$	$\begin{array}{r} \underline{} \\ +\ 54 \\ \hline \end{array}$
94	95		
$\begin{array}{r} 399 \\ +\ 466 \\ \hline \end{array}$	$\begin{array}{r} \underline{} \\ +\ 466 \\ \hline \end{array}$	$\begin{array}{r} 502 \\ +\ 264 \\ \hline \end{array}$	$\begin{array}{r} \underline{} \\ +\ 264 \\ \hline \end{array}$
$\begin{array}{r} 601 \\ +\ 385 \\ \hline \end{array}$	$\begin{array}{r} \underline{} \\ +\ 385 \\ \hline \end{array}$	$\begin{array}{r} 198 \\ +\ 727 \\ \hline \end{array}$	$\begin{array}{r} \underline{} \\ +\ 727 \\ \hline \end{array}$

Write equations to solve the word problem.

James wants to buy some sneakers for $99 and a basketball for $34.

Show an estimation of the total cost that he could do in his head, and then figure out the exact cost.

estimation

$ _____

+ _____

$

problem

$ _____

+ _____

$

Round and Subtract

You might use estimation with subtraction if you want to figure out the difference between two scores while at a game.

Estimate the difference by rounding to the nearest 10 or 100. Then solve the problems and compare the answer with the estimation. How close are they?

problem	estimation	problem	estimation
5 15 ~~65~~ − 29 **36**	65 − 30 **35**	74 − 29	74 − ___
526 − 301	526 − ___	482 − 198	482 − ___
724 − 502	724 − ___	963 − 599	963 − ___

Write equations to solve the word problem.

Ellie wants to buy a bag that costs $54. She plans to pay part of the cost using a gift card with $29 left on it.

Estimate the cost of the bag minus her gift-card money. Then figure out the exact cost.

estimation

$ _____

− _____

$ [ ]

problem

$ _____

− _____

$ [ ]

Add Three Numbers

You add three numbers the same way you add two numbers: add the ones column first, then the tens, and then the hundreds.

Solve the problems. Sometimes you'll need to use regrouping.

52	72	34	45
33	11	55	61
+ 4	+ 15	+ 2	+ 26
89			

600	502	720	420
40	24	30	23
+ 2	+ 3	+ 6	+ 5

352	223	274	439
500	349	283	628
+ 24	+ 21	+ 139	+ 682

452	823
303	233
+ 777	+ 523

Add to Subtract

One way to find the difference between two numbers is to figure out how much you need to add to the smaller number to reach the bigger number.

Use the number lines to help you solve the subtraction problems using addition.

number line	addition
762 – 427 = 335 +300 +30 +3 +2 427 727 757 760 762	300 30 3 + 2 —— 335
414 – 158 = ☐ 158 414	
627 – 339 = ☐ 339 627	
931 – 525 = ☐ 525 931	

What Is Multiplication?

Multiplication is repeated addition. The symbol x means **groups of**, or **times**.

Draw lines to match the addition and multiplication equations.

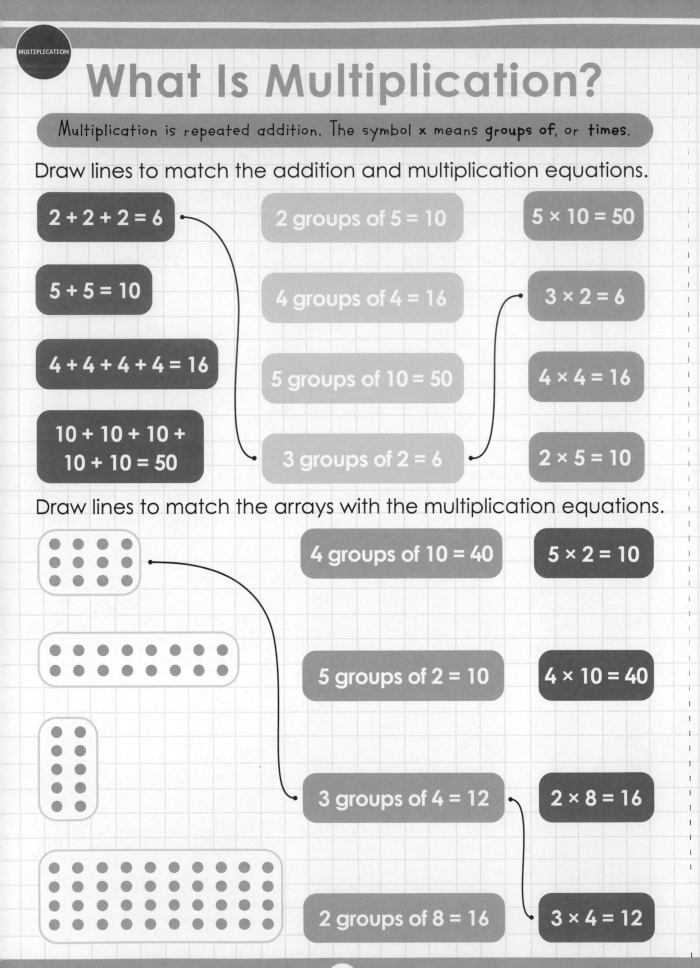

2 + 2 + 2 = 6	2 groups of 5 = 10	5 × 10 = 50
5 + 5 = 10	4 groups of 4 = 16	3 × 2 = 6
4 + 4 + 4 + 4 = 16	5 groups of 10 = 50	4 × 4 = 16
10 + 10 + 10 + 10 + 10 = 50	3 groups of 2 = 6	2 × 5 = 10

Draw lines to match the arrays with the multiplication equations.

4 groups of 10 = 40   5 × 2 = 10

5 groups of 2 = 10   4 × 10 = 40

3 groups of 4 = 12   2 × 8 = 16

2 groups of 8 = 16   3 × 4 = 12

Work with Arrays

You can multiply factors in any order and you'll still get the same answer. Knowing that 2 x 3 = 6 tells you that 3 x 2 = 6 as well.

Use the arrays to complete the equations.

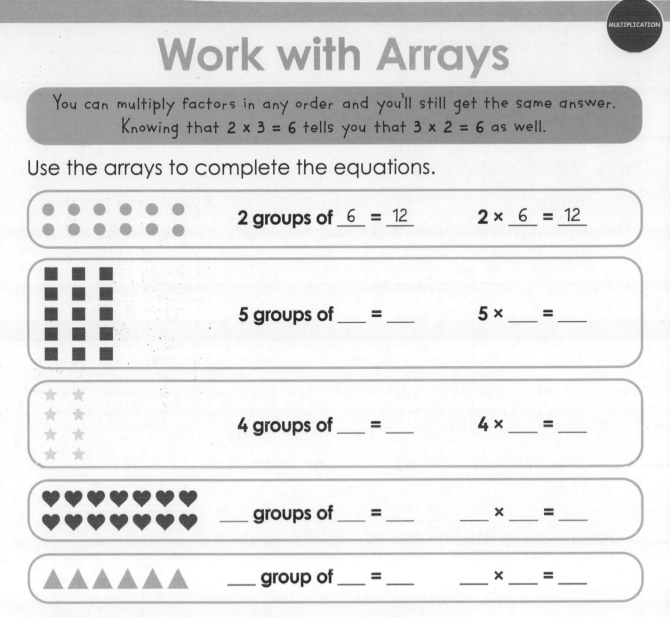

2 groups of _6_ = _12_   2 × _6_ = _12_

5 groups of ___ = ___   5 × ___ = ___

4 groups of ___ = ___   4 × ___ = ___

___ groups of ___ = ___   ___ × ___ = ___

___ group of ___ = ___   ___ × ___ = ___

Use the arrays to complete the equations.

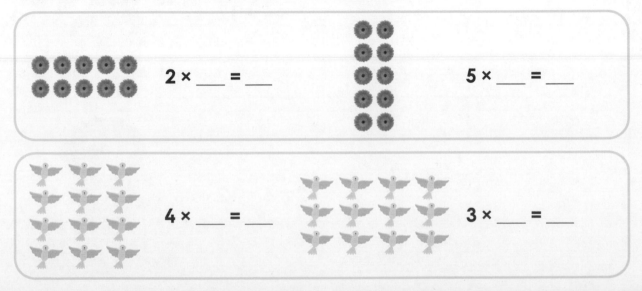

2 × ___ = ___   5 × ___ = ___

4 × ___ = ___   3 × ___ = ___

Use Grid Arrays

Arrays can be shown as **rows of dots** (or objects),
or they can be shown as a **grid** of squares.

Write the two multiplication facts that belong to each array.

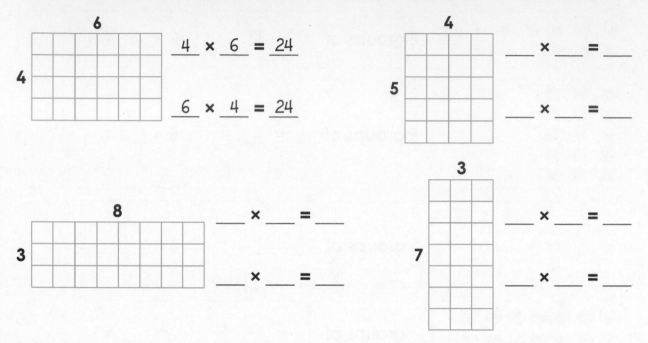

6

4

$\underline{4} \times \underline{6} = \underline{24}$

$\underline{6} \times \underline{4} = \underline{24}$

4

5

___ × ___ = ___

___ × ___ = ___

8

3

___ × ___ = ___

___ × ___ = ___

3

7

___ × ___ = ___

___ × ___ = ___

Draw an array that matches each equation.

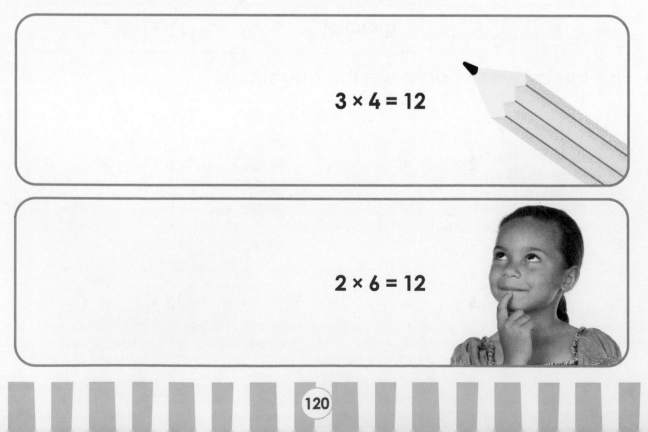

3 × 4 = 12

2 × 6 = 12

Multiply by 0 and 1

Zero groups of any number are always zero. 0 x 4 = 0.
One group of any number is always that number. 1 x 4 = 4.

Write the product in the box.

0 groups of 1 = 0	0 × 1 = 0
0 groups of 2 = 0	0 × 2 = 0
0 groups of 3 = ___	0 × 3 = ___
0 groups of 4 = ___	0 × 4 = ___
0 groups of 5 = ___	0 × 5 = ___
0 groups of 6 = ___	0 × 6 = ___
0 groups of 7 = ___	0 × 7 = ___
0 groups of 8 = ___	0 × 8 = ___
0 groups of 9 = ___	0 × 9 = ___
0 groups of 10 = ___	0 × 10 = ___

This means that 0 × 89 = ___

1 group of 1 = 1	1 × 1 = 1
1 group of 2 = 2	1 × 2 = 2
1 group of 3 = ___	1 × 3 = ___
1 group of 4 = ___	1 × 4 = ___
1 group of 5 = ___	1 × 5 = ___
1 group of 6 = ___	1 × 6 = ___
1 group of 7 = ___	1 × 7 = ___
1 group of 8 = ___	1 × 8 = ___
1 group of 9 = ___	1 × 9 = ___
1 group of 10 = ___	1 × 10 = ___

This means that 1 × 64 = ___

Fill in the missing factors.

___ × 6 = 6   ___ × 7 = 0   ___ × 9 = 0   ___ × 3 = 3

___ × 26 = 0   ___ × 73 = 73   ___ × 46 = 46   ___ × 38 = 0

Complete the equations. You can decide what factor to put in each problem.

0 × ___ = ___   1 × ___ = ___   0 × ___ = ___   1 × ___ = __

Multiply by 10

You can **skip count** to figure out the 10 times table. If you skip count by 10 for 4 numbers, you get 40, and 10 x 4 = 40.

There are 10 pencils in each pack. Skip count by 10 to solve the problems.

| 10 Pencils | 10 Pencils | 10 Pencils | 10 Pencils | 10 Pencils | 10 Pencils | 10 Pencils | 10 Pencils | 10 Pencils | 10 Pencils |

1 group of 10 = _____   1 × 10 = _____

2 groups of 10 = _____   2 × 10 = _____

3 groups of 10 = _____   3 × 10 = _____

4 groups of 10 = _____   4 × 10 = _____

5 groups of 10 = _____   5 × 10 = _____

6 groups of 10 = _____   6 × 10 = _____

7 groups of 10 = _____   7 × 10 = _____

8 groups of 10 = _____   8 × 10 = _____

9 groups of 10 = _____   9 × 10 = _____

10 groups of 10 = _____   10 × 10 = _____

This means that 10 × 56 = 560   and   10 × 47 = _____

Fill in the missing factors.

☐ × 5 = 50   ☐ × 7 = 70   ☐ × 10 = 20   ☐ × 1 = 10

☐ × 10 = 80   10 × ☐ = 30   ☐ × 6 = 60   10 × ☐ = 50

2 × ☐ = 20   ☐ × 10 = 40   9 × ☐ = 90   ☐ × 10 = 100

Multiply by 2 and 5

You can use your **doubles knowledge** to figure out the 2 times table.
6 + 6 = 12 and so 2 x 6 = 12.

Solve the problems.

1 + 1 = ____	and	2 × 1 = ____
2 + 2 = ____	and	2 × 2 = ____
3 + 3 = ____	and	2 × 3 = ____
4 + 4 = ____	and	2 × 4 = ____
5 + 5 = ____	and	2 × 5 = ____

6 + 6 = ____	and	2 × 6 = ____
7 + 7 = ____	and	2 × 7 = ____
8 + 8 = ____	and	2 × 8 = ____
9 + 9 = ____	and	2 × 9 = ____
10 + 10 = ____	and	2 × 10 = ____

All the numbers in the 5 times table end in 5 or 0.

Skip count by 5 to continue coloring the pattern.
Read the numbers aloud. Then solve the problems.

1	2	3	4	5	6	7	8	9	10
11	12	13	14	15	16	17	18	19	20
21	22	23	24	25	26	27	28	29	30
31	32	33	34	35	36	37	38	39	40
41	42	43	44	45	46	47	48	49	50

5 × 1 = ____   5 × 2 = ____

5 × 3 = ____   5 × 4 = ____

5 × 5 = ____   5 × 6 = ____

5 × 7 = ____   5 × 8 = ____

5 × 9 = ____   5 × 10 = ____

Complete the equations.

5 × 4 = ☐	4 × 5 = ☐	☐ × 4 = 20	☐ × 5 = 20
5 × 6 = ☐	6 × 5 = ☐	☐ × 5 = 30	☐ × 6 = 30
5 × 9 = ☐	9 × 5 = ☐	☐ × 9 = 45	☐ × 5 = 45

Multiply by 3 and 4

Use the flashcards at the back of the book to learn your times tables **by heart.** They'll keep helping you with math, even in high school.

Complete the pattern, adding 3 each time until you reach 30.

3, 6, 9, ___ , ___ ,18, ___ , ___ , ___ , 30

Use the pattern above to complete the 3 times table.

$3 \times 1 =$ ___ $3 \times 2 =$ ___ $3 \times 3 =$ ___ $3 \times 4 =$ ___ $3 \times 5 =$ ___

$3 \times 6 =$ ___ $3 \times 7 =$ ___ $3 \times 8 =$ ___ $3 \times 9 =$ ___ $3 \times 10 =$ ___

Complete the pattern, adding 4 each time until you reach 40.

4, 8, 12, ___ , 20, ___ , ___ , ___ , ___ , 40

Use the pattern above to complete the 4 times table.

$4 \times 1 =$ ___ $4 \times 2 =$ ___ $4 \times 3 =$ ___ $4 \times 4 =$ ___ $4 \times 5 =$ ___

$4 \times 6 =$ ___ $4 \times 7 =$ ___ $4 \times 8 =$ ___ $4 \times 9 =$ ___ $4 \times 10 =$ ___

Cover the answers above and solve the problems.
Circle the ones you didn't already know.

$4 \times 4 =$ $4 \times 9 =$ $3 \times 1 =$ $4 \times 8 =$

$3 \times 6 =$ $4 \times 10 =$ $3 \times 4 =$ $4 \times 6 =$

$4 \times 2 =$ $3 \times 5 =$ $4 \times 5 =$ $3 \times 9 =$

$3 \times 7 =$ $3 \times 8 =$ $4 \times 7 =$ $3 \times 3 =$

Multiply by 6 and 7

Remember, you **already know** many of these. You know 2 x 6 = 12, so you also know 6 x 2 = 12.

Complete the pattern, adding 6 each time until you reach 60.

6, 12, 18, ___ , ___ , 36, ___ , ___ , ___ , 60

Use the pattern above to complete the 6 times table.

6 × 1 = ___	6 × 2 = ___	6 × 3 = ___	6 × 4 = ___	6 × 5 = ___
6 × 6 = ___	6 × 7 = ___	6 × 8 = ___	6 × 9 = ___	6 × 10 = ___

Complete the pattern, adding 7 each time until you reach 70.

7, 14, ___ , 28, ___ , 42, ___ , ___ , ___ , 70

Use the pattern above to complete the 7 times table.

7 × 1 = ___	7 × 2 = ___	7 × 3 = ___	7 × 4 = ___	7 × 5 = ___
7 × 6 = ___	7 × 7 = ___	7 × 8 = ___	7 × 9 = ___	7 × 10 = ___

Cover the answers above and solve the problems.
Circle the ones you didn't already know.

7 × 8 = ☐	6 × 4 = ☐	7 × 2 = ☐	7 × 4 = ☐
7 × 9 = ☐	6 × 3 = ☐	6 × 8 = ☐	6 × 6 = ☐
7 × 6 = ☐	6 × 2 = ☐	7 × 3 = ☐	7 × 7 = ☐
7 × 10 = ☐	6 × 9 = ☐	7 × 5 = ☐	6 × 5 = ☐

Multiply by 8 and 9

If you know 4 x 3 = 12, you can **double it** to figure out 8 x 3.
That's because 8 is double 4. So, 8 x 3 = 24.

Complete the pattern, adding 8 each time until you reach 80.

8 , 16 , ___ , 32 , ___ , ___ , 56, ___ , ___ , 80

Use the pattern above to complete the 8 times table.

8 × 1 = ___   8 × 2 = ___   8 × 3 = ___   8 × 4 = ___   8 × 5 = ___

8 × 6 = ___   8 × 7 = ___   8 × 8 = ___   8 × 9 = ___   8 × 10 = ___

Cover the answers above and solve the problems.
Circle the ones you didn't already know.

8 × 2 = ☐   8 × 7 = ☐   8 × 6 = ☐   8 × 3 = ☐

8 × 9 = ☐   8 × 8 = ☐   8 × 4 = ☐   8 × 5 = ☐

The digits in 9 times-table products all add up to 9.
For example, 4 x 9 = 36, and 3 + 6 equals 9.

Complete the pattern, adding 9 each time until you reach 90.

9, ___ , 27, ___ , ___ , 54, ___ , ___ , ___ , 90

9 × 1 = ___   9 × 2 = ___   9 × 3 = ___   9 × 4 = ___   9 × 5 = ___

9 × 6 = ___   9 × 7 = ___   9 × 8 = ___   9 × 9 = ___   9 × 10 = ___

Does the sum of the digits always add up to nine? **Yes / No**
Now look for other helpful patterns in your list of answers.

Missing Factors

Remember, the numbers you multiply are called **factors**, and the answer is called the **product**.

Fill in the missing factors.

$2 \times \boxed{} = 14$ $\boxed{} \times 7 = 14$ $6 \times \boxed{} = 42$ $\boxed{} \times 8 = 64$

$\boxed{} \times 4 = 4$ $3 \times \boxed{} = 27$ $\boxed{} \times 5 = 25$ $7 \times \boxed{} = 49$

$9 \times \boxed{} = 54$ $\boxed{} \times 8 = 80$ $9 \times \boxed{} = 18$ $\boxed{} \times 4 = 24$

$\boxed{} \times 6 = 18$ $8 \times \boxed{} = 32$ $\boxed{} \times 10 = 50$ $1 \times \boxed{} = 9$

$7 \times \boxed{} = 21$ $\boxed{} \times 7 = 35$ $9 \times \boxed{} = 63$ $\boxed{} \times 8 = 48$

Write equations to solve the problems. Circle the answers.

Aubrey has 18 pieces of candy. She wants to share them evenly among 2 friends and herself. How many pieces will each friend get?

$\boxed{} \times \boxed{} = 18$

Logan has $45. He wants to spend it all on paints. Each tube of paint costs $5. How many tubes can he afford?

$\$ \boxed{} \times \boxed{} = \$ 45$

Multi-Step Problems

With long problems, solve the part inside the **parentheses first**. Then solve any multiplication, and finally solve any addition or subtraction.

Solve the problems.

$5 + (3 \times 2) = \boxed{}$

$(7 \times 6) + 30 = \boxed{}$

$6 + (10 \times 6) = \boxed{}$

$(5 \times 2) \times 3 = \boxed{}$

$(2 \times 3) \times 6 = \boxed{}$

$(9 \times 6) - 4 = \boxed{}$

$(4 \times 2) + 4 = \boxed{}$

$4 \times (2 + 4) = \boxed{}$

$(3 + 5) \times 3 = \boxed{}$

$(6 \times 6) + 200 = \boxed{}$

$555 - (2 \times 5) = \boxed{}$

$(10 \times 10) - 30 = \boxed{}$

$(10 - 4) \times 8 + 2 = \boxed{}$

$(4 \times 2) \times 5 + 6 = \boxed{}$

$4 \times (2 \times 5) - 5 = \boxed{}$

Write equations to solve the problems. Circle the answers.

Dad buys 3 bags of apples. Each bag holds 6 apples. He then buys 2 more loose apples. How many apples does he buy altogether?

$(\boxed{} \times \boxed{}) + \boxed{} = \boxed{}$

Mom buys 4 packets of cookies. Each packet holds 10 cookies. At home, she finds that 2 of the cookies are broken. How many whole cookies does she have left?

$(\boxed{} \times \boxed{}) - \boxed{} = \boxed{}$

Two-Digit Multiplication

You can break a hard problem into **two easy ones**.
3 x 14 can be broken into 3 x 10 and 3 x 4.

Color the arrays to match the colors in the equations.
Then solve the problems. The first one has been done for you.

4 × 13 = (4 × 10) + (4 × 3) = 40 + 12 = <u>52</u>

3 × 13 = (3 × 10) + (3 × 3) = 30 + 9 = ___

5 × 15 = (5 × 10) + (5 × 5) = ___ + ___ = ___

Solve the problems using multiplication and addition.

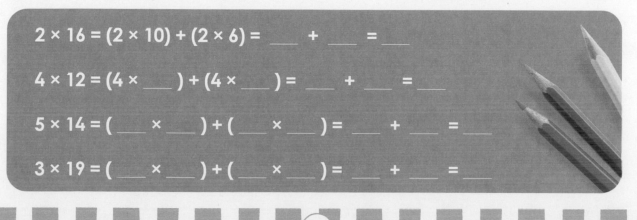

2 × 16 = (2 × 10) + (2 × 6) = ___ + ___ = ___

4 × 12 = (4 × ___) + (4 × ___) = ___ + ___ = ___

5 × 14 = (___ × ___) + (___ × ___) = ___ + ___ = ___

3 × 19 = (___ × ___) + (___ × ___) = ___ + ___ = ___

Column Multiplication

To multiply **two-digit numbers**, multiply the digit in the 1s column first.
Then multiply the digit in the 10s column.

Solve the problems.

5	7	9	8
× 8	× 6	× 2	× 7
40			

4	9	6	10
× 8	× 4	× 6	× 3

Solve the problems.

64	32	46	83
× 2	× 3	× 1	× 3
128			

72	51	94	60
× 4	× 5	× 2	× 5

Write an equation to solve the word problem.

Mrs. Green has 4 children.
If a child's coat costs $42,
how much will it cost her
to buy them all new coats?

$ _____

× _____

$42

Use Regrouping

> If a product is **above** 9, put the 1s digit in the answer line and the 10s digit above the 10s column. Add this number to the 10s column product.

Use regrouping to solve the problems.

100s	10s	1s
	1	
	4	3
×		6
2	5	8

100s	10s	1s
	2	8
×		3

100s	10s	1s
	3	6
×		2

100s	10s	1s
	8	2
×		5

100s	10s	1s
	9	3
×		4

100s	10s	1s
	6	2
×		7

Use regrouping to solve the problems. This time, imagine the place-value columns above the digits.

2
36
× 4
144

35
× 7

72
× 6

66
× 4

52
× 9

48
× 5

92
× 3

55
× 3

88
× 3

Three-Digit Multiplication

Remember that multiplication is the same as **repeated addition** of the same number.

Use addition and multiplication to solve the problem pairs.

```
        523          523              621          621
        523        ×   3              621        ×   4
      + 523                           621
                                    + 621
```

Use addition and multiplication to solve the problem pairs.
This time you will need to use regrouping. Show your work.

```
   21
  386          21              978          978
  386         386            + 978        ×   2
+ 386       ×   3
 1,158        1,158
```

```
  371          371              433          433
  371        ×   3              433        ×   4
+ 371                           433
                              + 433
```

Which did you find easier, addition or multiplication?

_____

Three-Digit Multiplication

If a product is zero, be sure to put a 0 in the correct place-value column. Zero is a **placeholder**.

Solve the problems. Show your work.

700	620	801	400	503
× 2	× 4	× 7	× 9	× 3
1,400				

580	604	500	630
× 6	× 2	× 7	× 5

Solve the problems. Show your work.

21				
$374	$723	$462	$705	$289
× 4	× 6	× 7	× 3	× 9
$1,496				

$629	$830	$729	$632
× 6	× 5	× 1	× 4

Write an equation to solve the word problem.

A train trip costs $160 per ticket.

How much would it cost for 4 tickets?

$ _____

× _____

133

Make Estimates

In a store, you can estimate the cost of multiple items in your head to get a **rough idea** of how much you'll pay.

Estimate the product by rounding to the nearest 10. Then solve the problem and compare the answer with the estimation. How close are they?

problem	estimation	problem	estimation
8 59 × 9 531	60 × 9 540	31 × 6 186	30 × 6 180
62 × 7	___ × 7	49 × 5	___ × 5
48 × 8	___ × 8	72 × 5	___ × 5

Solve the word problem.

A teacher sees that basketballs cost $49 each. She wants to buy 4 for her class.

Show an estimation of the cost that she could do in her head, and then figure out the exact cost.

estimation

$ _____
× _____
$

problem

$ _____
× _____
$

Greater, Less Than, or Equal

Remember that < means **less than** and that > means **greater than**.

Write <, >, or = in each box.

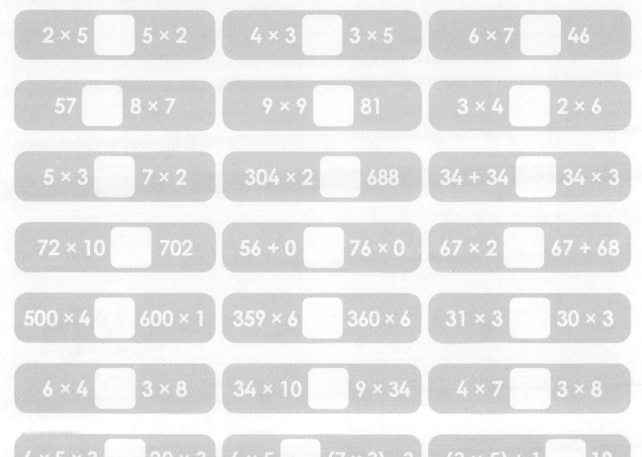

2×5 ☐ 5×2 4×3 ☐ 3×5 6×7 ☐ 46

57 ☐ 8×7 9×9 ☐ 81 3×4 ☐ 2×6

5×3 ☐ 7×2 304×2 ☐ 688 $34 + 34$ ☐ 34×3

72×10 ☐ 702 $56 + 0$ ☐ 76×0 67×2 ☐ $67 + 68$

500×4 ☐ 600×1 359×6 ☐ 360×6 31×3 ☐ 30×3

6×4 ☐ 3×8 34×10 ☐ 9×34 4×7 ☐ 3×8

$4 \times 5 \times 3$ ☐ 20×3 4×5 ☐ $(7 \times 3) - 3$ $(3 \times 5) + 1$ ☐ 18

Solve the problems. Show your work.

Each book in Noah's favorite series costs $5. A boxed set of all 8 books costs $32. Is it cheaper to buy the books individually or as a boxed set?

_____

At Value Mart, a pack of 4 T-shirts costs $12.
At Bargain Mart, you can buy 2 T-shirts for $6.
Which store, if either, offers the cheapest price per T-shirt?

_____

Word Problems

To solve a word problem, figure out what **equation** goes with it.
Then solve the equation.

Write equations to solve the problems. Circle the answers.

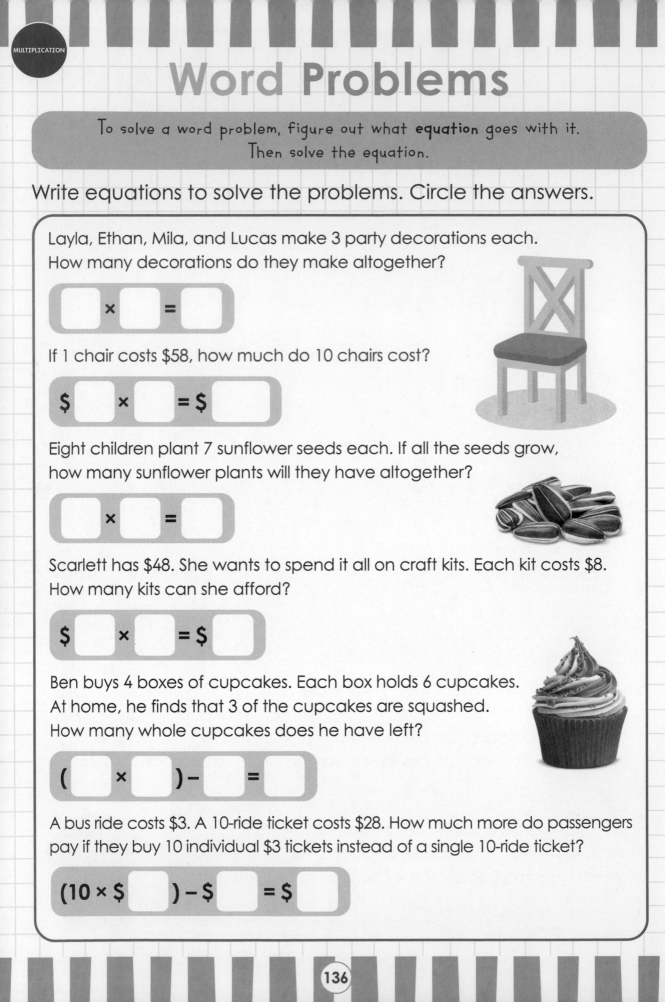

Layla, Ethan, Mila, and Lucas make 3 party decorations each.
How many decorations do they make altogether?

☐ × ☐ = ☐

If 1 chair costs $58, how much do 10 chairs cost?

$ ☐ × ☐ = $ ☐

Eight children plant 7 sunflower seeds each. If all the seeds grow,
how many sunflower plants will they have altogether?

☐ × ☐ = ☐

Scarlett has $48. She wants to spend it all on craft kits. Each kit costs $8.
How many kits can she afford?

$ ☐ × ☐ = $ ☐

Ben buys 4 boxes of cupcakes. Each box holds 6 cupcakes.
At home, he finds that 3 of the cupcakes are squashed.
How many whole cupcakes does he have left?

(☐ × ☐) − ☐ = ☐

A bus ride costs $3. A 10-ride ticket costs $28. How much more do passengers
pay if they buy 10 individual $3 tickets instead of a single 10-ride ticket?

(10 × $ ☐) − $ ☐ = $ ☐

Tables Practice

Times tables are easier to remember if you **practice** them regularly.

Fill in the missing numbers. The middle number is multiplied by the factor in the center. The product goes in the outer ring.

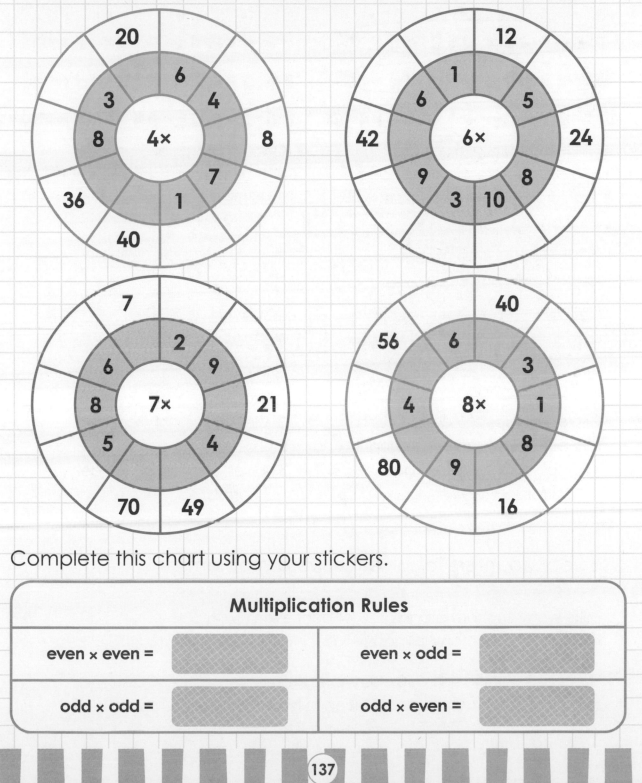

Complete this chart using your stickers.

Multiplication Rules			
even × even =		even × odd =	
odd × odd =		odd × even =	

What Is Division?

Division is splitting, or breaking up, a number into **equal-sized smaller numbers**. The symbol ÷ means **divided by** or **shared between**.

Use the example to help you complete the problems.

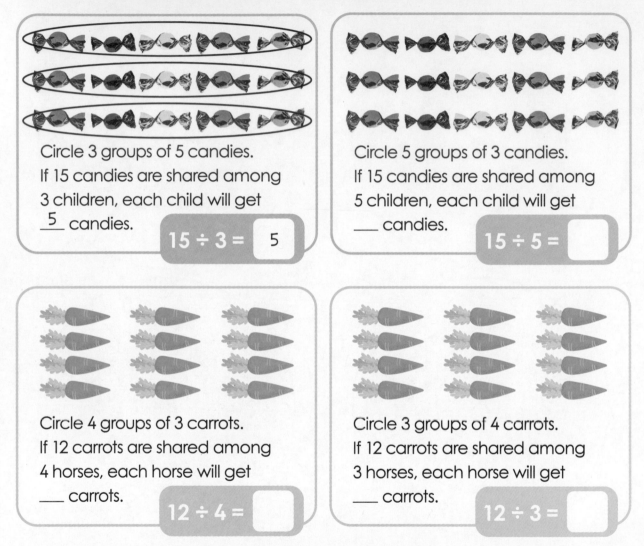

Circle 3 groups of 5 candies.
If 15 candies are shared among
3 children, each child will get
_5_ candies.

$15 \div 3 = 5$

Circle 5 groups of 3 candies.
If 15 candies are shared among
5 children, each child will get
___ candies.

$15 \div 5 =$

Circle 4 groups of 3 carrots.
If 12 carrots are shared among
4 horses, each horse will get
___ carrots.

$12 \div 4 =$

Circle 3 groups of 4 carrots.
If 12 carrots are shared among
3 horses, each horse will get
___ carrots.

$12 \div 3 =$

Use your counters to solve the word problems.

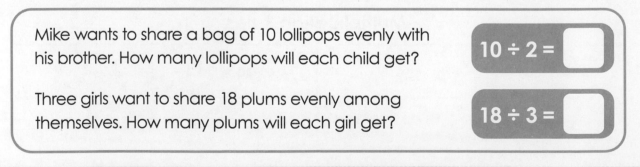

Mike wants to share a bag of 10 lollipops evenly with his brother. How many lollipops will each child get?

$10 \div 2 =$

Three girls want to share 18 plums evenly among themselves. How many plums will each girl get?

$18 \div 3 =$

Subtraction and Division

You can divide a number into equal amounts by subtracting the same amount each time.

Show the jumps on the number lines and solve the problems.

```
  -3     -3     -3     -3     -3     -3     -3
0 1 2 3 4 5 6 7 8 9 10 11 12 13 14 15 16 17 18 19 20 21 22 23 24 25
```

How many times can you subtract 3 from 21?
It took __7__ jumps to reach 0.

This means $21 \div 3 =$ [7]

```
0 1 2 3 4 5 6 7 8 9 10 11 12 13 14 15 16 17 18 19 20
```

How many times can you subtract 6 from 18?
It took ___ jumps to reach 0.

This means $18 \div 6 =$ [ ]

```
0 1 2 3 4 5 6 7 8 9 10 11 12 13 14 15 16 17 18 19 20 21 22 23 24 25
```

How many times can you subtract 7 from 21?
It took ___ jumps to reach 0.

This means $21 \div 7 =$ [ ]

```
0 1 2 3 4 5 6 7 8 9 10 11 12 13 14 15 16 17 18 19 20
```

How many times can you subtract 5 from 20?
It took ___ jumps to reach 0.

This means $20 \div 5 =$ [ ]

Count how many times each number is subtracted to help you solve the division problems.

$10 - 2 - 2 - 2 - 2 - 2 =$ __0__
$10 \div 2 =$ __5__

$32 - 8 - 8 - 8 - 8 =$ ___
$32 \div 8 =$ ___

$27 - 9 - 9 - 9 =$ ___
$27 \div 9 =$ ___

$6 - 2 - 2 - 2 =$ ___
$6 \div 2 =$ ___

Multiplication and Division

Multiplication and division are **opposite operations**. This means that if you know your times tables, you also know your division facts.

Sticker the answers to the problems in the correct boxes.

How many balls are in 3 groups of 4?

$3 \times 4 = \boxed{12}$

If you divide 12 balls into 3 groups, how many are in each group?

$12 \div 3 = \boxed{4}$

How many balls are in 4 groups of 6?

$6 \times 4 =$

If you divide 24 balls into 4 groups, how many are in each group?

$24 \div 4 =$

How many balls are in 7 groups of 3?

$7 \times 3 =$

If you divide 21 balls into 7 groups, how many are in each group?

$21 \div 7 =$

Use your times-table knowledge to complete the fact families.

$7 \times 6 = \underline{42}$	$6 \times 7 = \underline{42}$	$42 \div 7 = \underline{6}$	$42 \div 6 = \underline{7}$
$10 \times 3 = \underline{\hphantom{0}}$	$3 \times 10 = \underline{\hphantom{0}}$	$30 \div 3 = \underline{\hphantom{0}}$	$30 \div 10 = \underline{\hphantom{0}}$
$6 \times 9 = \underline{\hphantom{0}}$	$9 \times 6 = \underline{\hphantom{0}}$	$54 \div 6 = \underline{\hphantom{0}}$	$54 \div 9 = \underline{\hphantom{0}}$
$6 \times 8 = \underline{\hphantom{0}}$	$8 \times 6 = \underline{\hphantom{0}}$	$48 \div 6 = \underline{\hphantom{0}}$	$48 \div 8 = \underline{\hphantom{0}}$

Divide by 2

When you divide a number by 2, you divide it in **half**.
For example, 10 ÷ 2 = 5, and half of 10 is 5.

Circle 2 equal groups in each array. Then fill in the gaps.

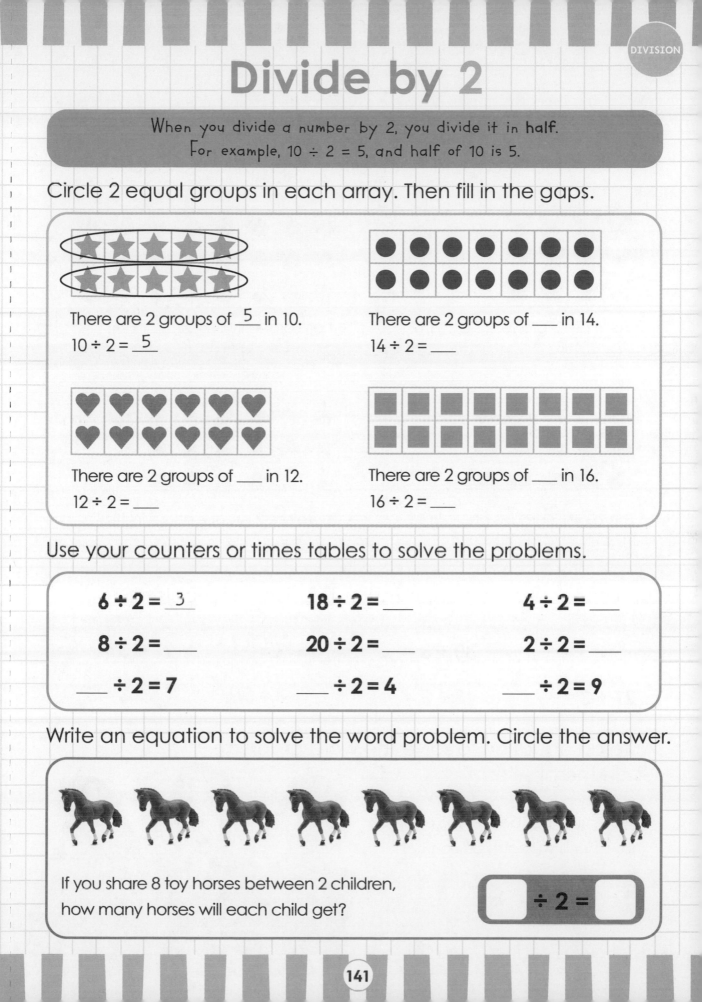

There are 2 groups of _5_ in 10.
10 ÷ 2 = _5_

There are 2 groups of ___ in 14.
14 ÷ 2 = ___

There are 2 groups of ___ in 12.
12 ÷ 2 = ___

There are 2 groups of ___ in 16.
16 ÷ 2 = ___

Use your counters or times tables to solve the problems.

6 ÷ 2 = _3_	18 ÷ 2 = ___	4 ÷ 2 = ___
8 ÷ 2 = ___	20 ÷ 2 = ___	2 ÷ 2 = ___
___ ÷ 2 = 7	___ ÷ 2 = 4	___ ÷ 2 = 9

Write an equation to solve the word problem. Circle the answer.

If you share 8 toy horses between 2 children,
how many horses will each child get?

___ ÷ 2 = ___

Divide by 3

The answer to a division problem is called the **quotient**.

Circle 3 equal groups in each array. Then fill in the gaps.

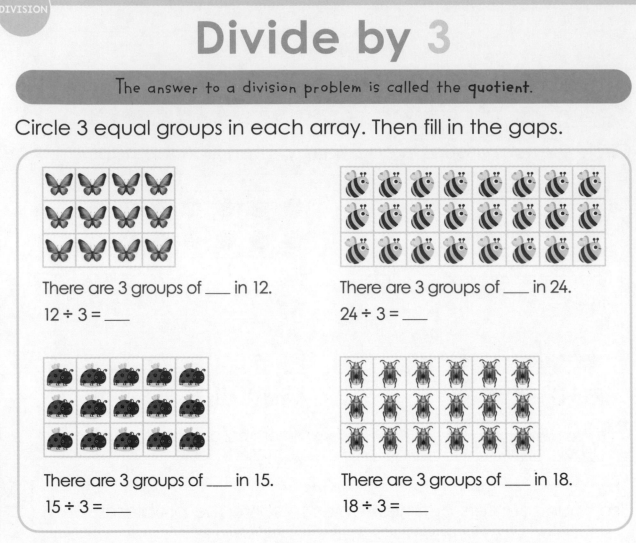

There are 3 groups of ___ in 12.

12 ÷ 3 = ___

There are 3 groups of ___ in 24.

24 ÷ 3 = ___

There are 3 groups of ___ in 15.

15 ÷ 3 = ___

There are 3 groups of ___ in 18.

18 ÷ 3 = ___

Use your counters or times tables to solve the problems.

6 ÷ 3 = ___   30 ÷ 3 = ___   9 ÷ 3 = ___   21 ÷ 3 = ___

27 ÷ 3 = ___   3 ÷ 3 = ___   ___ ÷ 3 = 5   ___ ÷ 3 = 3

Write an equation to solve the word problem.
Circle the answer.

If you share $27 between 3 people,
how much will each person get?

$ [ ]   ÷ 3 = $ [ ]

Divide by 4

If you know your **times tables** by heart, you will find division much easier.

Circle 4 equal groups in each array. Then fill in the gaps.

There are 4 groups of ___ in 20.

20 ÷ 4 = ___

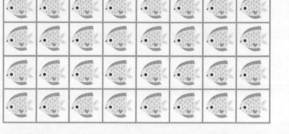

There are 4 groups of ___ in 32.

32 ÷ 4 = ___

There are 4 groups of ___ in 12.

12 ÷ 4 = ___

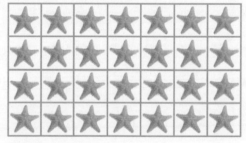

There are 4 groups of ___ in 28.

28 ÷ 4 = ___

Use your counters or times tables to solve the problems.

8 ÷ 4 = ___   36 ÷ 4 = ___   16 ÷ 4 = ___   24 ÷ 4 = ___

4 ÷ 4 = ___   40 ÷ 4 = ___   ___ ÷ 4 = 6   ___ ÷ 4 = 8

Write an equation to solve the word problem. Circle the answer.

If you share 16 treats between 4 dogs,
how many treats does each dog get?

[ ] ÷ 4 = [ ]

Divide by 5

The large number that is divided up is called the **dividend**. In 35 ÷ 5 = 7, the dividend is 35.

Circle 5 equal groups in each array. Then fill in the gaps.

There are 5 groups of ___ in 10.

10 ÷ 5 = ___

There are 5 groups of ___ in 15.

15 ÷ 5 = ___

There are 5 groups of ___ in 35.

35 ÷ 5 = ___

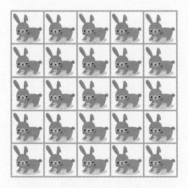

There are 5 groups of ___ in 25.

25 ÷ 5 = ___

Use your times-table knowledge to solve the problems.

45 ÷ 5 = ___   40 ÷ 5 = ___   30 ÷ 5 = ___   5 ÷ 5 = ___

20 ÷ 5 = ___   50 ÷ 5 = ___   ___ ÷ 5 = 4   ___ ÷ 5 = 7

Write an equation to solve the word problem. Circle the answer.

If you share 30 comic books between 5 children, how many comics does each child get?

☐ ÷ 5 = ☐

Divide by 6

The number by which the dividend is divided is called the **divisor**.
In 42 ÷ 6 = 7, the divisor is 6.

Circle 6 equal groups in each array. Then fill in the gaps.

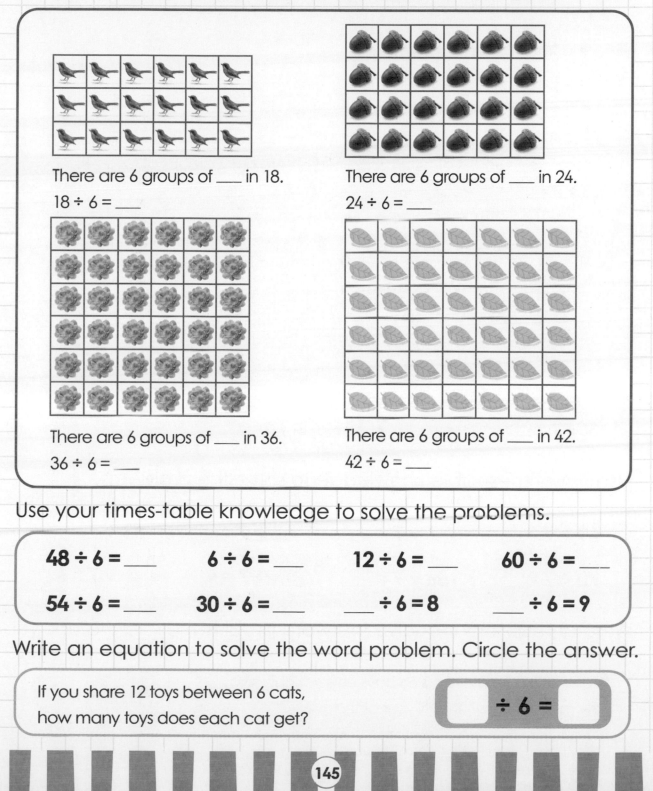

There are 6 groups of ___ in 18.

18 ÷ 6 = ___

There are 6 groups of ___ in 24.

24 ÷ 6 = ___

There are 6 groups of ___ in 36.

36 ÷ 6 = ___

There are 6 groups of ___ in 42.

42 ÷ 6 = ___

Use your times-table knowledge to solve the problems.

48 ÷ 6 = ___   6 ÷ 6 = ___   12 ÷ 6 = ___   60 ÷ 6 = ___

54 ÷ 6 = ___   30 ÷ 6 = ___   ___ ÷ 6 = 8   ___ ÷ 6 = 9

Write an equation to solve the word problem. Circle the answer.

If you share 12 toys between 6 cats,
how many toys does each cat get?

☐ ÷ 6 = ☐

Divide by 7

Think of division as **sharing**. Each person must get the same amount for it to be fair and correct.

Circle 7 equal groups in each array. Then fill in the gaps.

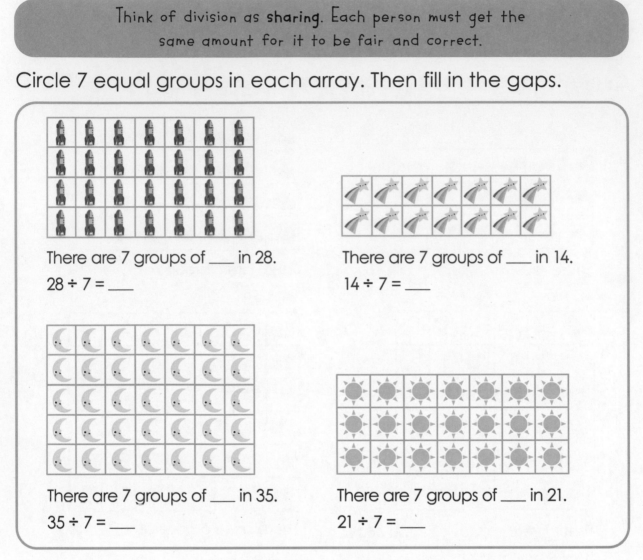

There are 7 groups of ___ in 28.

28 ÷ 7 = ___

There are 7 groups of ___ in 14.

14 ÷ 7 = ___

There are 7 groups of ___ in 35.

35 ÷ 7 = ___

There are 7 groups of ___ in 21.

21 ÷ 7 = ___

Use your times-table knowledge to solve the problems.

49 ÷ 7 = ___   7 ÷ 7 = ___   42 ÷ 7 = ___   63 ÷ 7 = ___

70 ÷ 7 = ___   56 ÷ 7 = ___   ___ ÷ 7 = 4   ___ ÷ 7 = 6

Write an equation to solve the word problem. Circle the answer.

A full week is 7 days. If it is 56 days until your birthday, how many weeks is it until your birthday?

[ ] ÷ 7 = [ ]

Divide by 8

Dividing by 8 is the **same** as dividing by 2 and then 4.
For example, 40 ÷ 2 = 20 and 20 ÷ 4 = 5. This means 40 ÷ 8 = 5.

Circle 8 equal groups in each array. Then fill in the gaps.

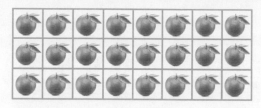

There are 8 groups of ___ in 24.

24 ÷ 8 = ___

There are 8 groups of ___ in 16.

16 ÷ 8 = ___

There are 8 groups of ___ in 40.

40 ÷ 8 = ___

There are 8 groups of ___ in 32.

32 ÷ 8 = ___

Use your times-table knowledge to solve the problems.

64 ÷ 8 = ___   56 ÷ 8 = ___   72 ÷ 8 = ___   48 ÷ 8 = ___

80 ÷ 8 = ___   8 ÷ 8 = ___   ___ ÷ 8 = 6   ___ ÷ 8 = 1

Write an equation to solve the word problem. Circle the answer.

If you share 48 seeds between 8 plant pots,
how many seeds will go in each pot?

[___] ÷ 8 = [___]

Divide by 9

For numbers that divide evenly by 9 and are equal to 90 or less, the answer is the number that is one more than the digit in the 10s position.

Circle 9 equal groups in each array. Then fill in the gaps.

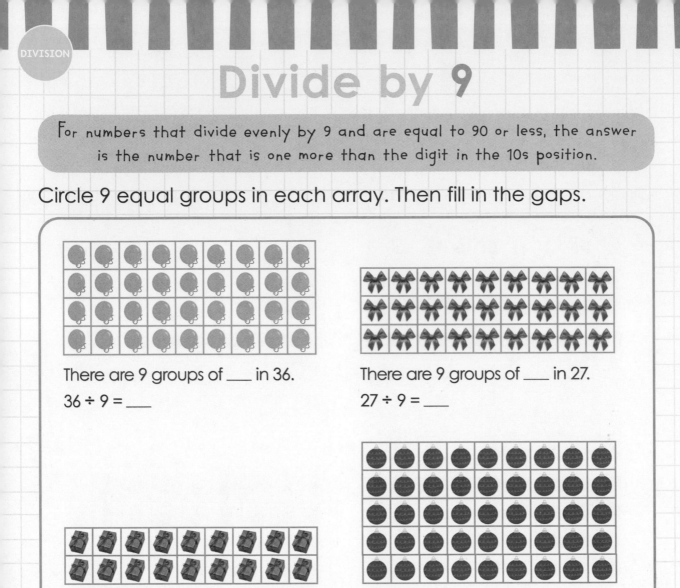

There are 9 groups of ___ in 36.

36 ÷ 9 = ___

There are 9 groups of ___ in 27.

27 ÷ 9 = ___

There are 9 groups of ___ in 18.

18 ÷ 9 = ___

There are 9 groups of ___ in 45.

45 ÷ 9 = ___

Use your times-table knowledge to solve the problems.

9 ÷ 9 = ___   72 ÷ 9 = ___   81 ÷ 9 = ___   54 ÷ 9 = ___

90 ÷ 9 = ___   63 ÷ 9 = ___   ___ ÷ 9 = 4   ___ ÷ 9 = 9

Write an equation to solve the word problem. Circle the answer.

If you cut a 72-meter rope into 9 equal-length pieces, how long will each piece be?

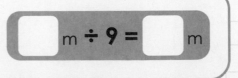

m ÷ 9 = [   ] m

Divide by 10

When you divide by ten, each digit moves down one place-value position.
For example, 260 ÷ 10 = 26, and 300 ÷ 10 = 30.

Solve the problems.

20 ÷ 10 = ☐   80 ÷ 10 = ☐   30 ÷ 10 = ☐   50 ÷ 10 = ☐

100 ÷ 10 = ☐   40 ÷ 10 = ☐   10 ÷ 10 = ☐   70 ÷ 10 = ☐

90 ÷ 10 = ☐   60 ÷ 10 = ☐   ☐ ÷ 10 = 6   ☐ ÷ 10 = 10

Use your place-value knowledge to solve the problems.

340 ÷ 10 = ☐   480 ÷ 10 = ☐   500 ÷ 10 = ☐   3,200 ÷ 10 = ☐

280 ÷ 10 = ☐   200 ÷ 10 = ☐   720 ÷ 10 = ☐   1,500 ÷ 10 = ☐

Use your place-value knowledge to solve the problem.

If you cut a 500 cm ribbon into 10 equal pieces, how long will each piece of ribbon be?

☐ cm ÷ 10 = ☐ cm

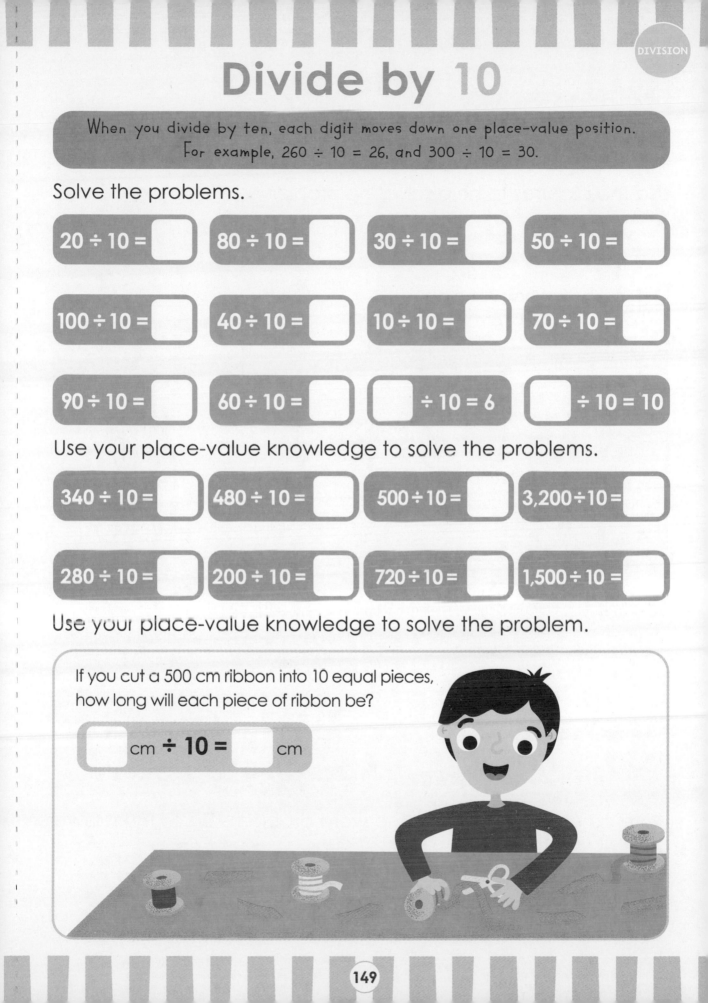

Divide by 1

Any number divided into groups of 1 will have that number of groups. For example, 5 ÷ 1 = 5.

Use the pictures to help solve the problems.

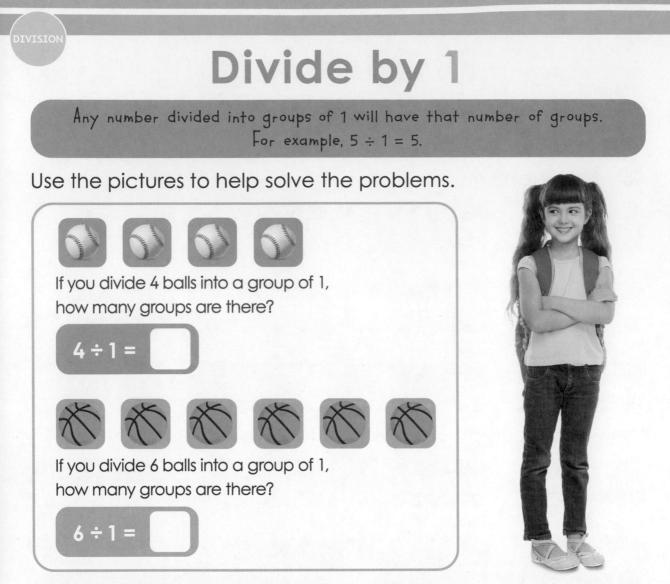

If you divide 4 balls into a group of 1, how many groups are there?

4 ÷ 1 = ☐

If you divide 6 balls into a group of 1, how many groups are there?

6 ÷ 1 = ☐

Solve the problems.

2 ÷ 1 = ___   6 ÷ 1 = ___   10 ÷ 1 = ___   17 ÷ 1 = ___

73 ÷ 1 = ___   1 ÷ 1 = ___   64 ÷ 1 = ___   37 ÷ 1 = ___

90 ÷ 1 = ___   60 ÷ 1 = ___   989 ÷ 1 = ___   7,336 ÷ 1 = ___

Write an equation to solve the word problem. Circle the answer.

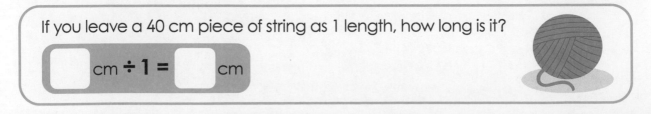

If you leave a 40 cm piece of string as 1 length, how long is it?

☐ cm ÷ 1 = ☐ cm

A New Layout

You can display division problems in different ways.
Whichever **layout** you use, the answer stays the same.

Draw lines to match the division equations.

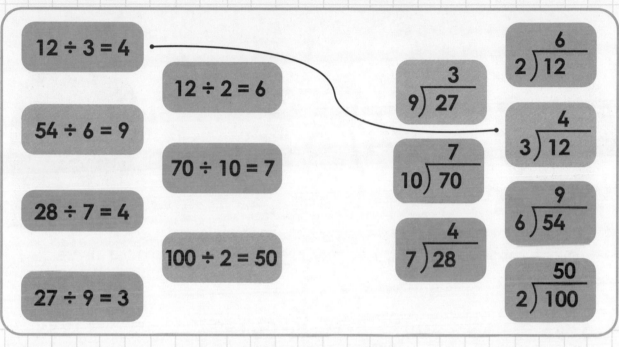

Write the answer above the ones column.

$8\overline{)48}$ $4\overline{)16}$ $3\overline{)12}$ $9\overline{)63}$

$4\overline{)28}$ $7\overline{)42}$ $3\overline{)27}$ $6\overline{)18}$

Write equations to solve the word problems. Circle the answers.

How many times does 3 go into 15?

_____

How many times does 4 go into 24?

_____

High Dividends

Read the speech bubbles. They show you how to divide numbers higher than those in your times tables.

How many times does 4 go into 6? It goes 1 time, with 2 left over.

How many times does 4 go into 28? It goes 7 times.

$$17$$
$$4\overline{)6^28}$$

Solve the problems. You will need to carry over most times.

$5\overline{)65}$ $\qquad$ $3\overline{)72}$ $\qquad$ $4\overline{)92}$ $\qquad$ $7\overline{)98}$

$6\overline{)84}$ $\qquad$ $2\overline{)36}$ $\qquad$ $3\overline{)63}$ $\qquad$ $6\overline{)72}$

$4\overline{)52}$ $\qquad$ $2\overline{)86}$ $\qquad$ $8\overline{)88}$ $\qquad$ $6\overline{)90}$

Write equations to solve the word problems. Circle the answers.

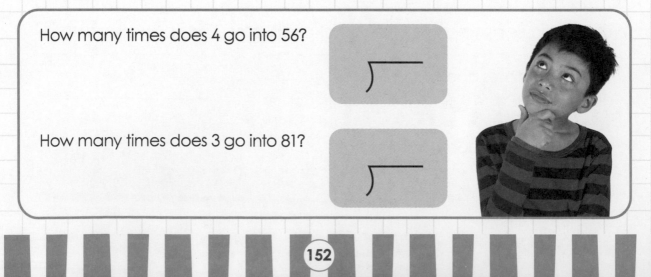

How many times does 4 go into 56?

How many times does 3 go into 81?

Multi-Step Problems

With long problems, solve the part inside the **parentheses first**. Then solve any division or multiplication, and then any addition or subtraction.

Solve the problems.

$(10 ÷ 2) + 4 =$ ____

$(30 ÷ 3) + 30 =$ ____

$7 + (21 ÷ 3) =$ ____

$(20 ÷ 4) × 2 =$ ____

$(2 × 6) ÷ 4 =$ ____

$(5 × 6) ÷ 3 =$ ____

$(9 ÷ 3) + 4 =$ ____

$4 × (15 ÷ 3) =$ ____

$(24 + 6) ÷ 3 =$ ____

$(25 ÷ 5) + 250 =$ ____

$888 - (14 ÷ 2) =$ ____

$(100 ÷ 10) + 43 =$ ____

$(35 ÷ 7) × 5 + 4 =$ ____

$(54 ÷ 9) × 5 + 6 =$ ____

$4 × (56 ÷ 8) - 5 =$ ____

$(81 ÷ 9) × 2 + 2 =$ ____

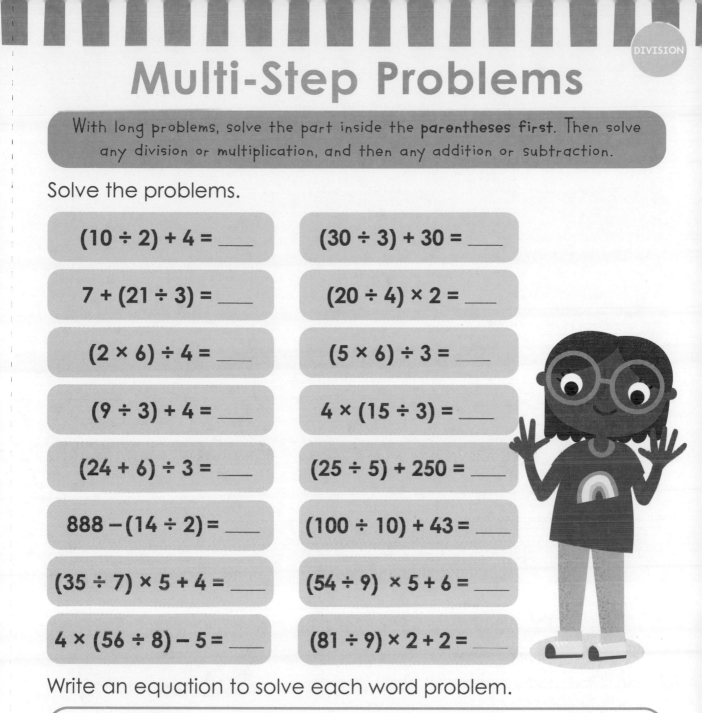

Write an equation to solve each word problem.

Grandpa shares a bag of 16 mandarins between 4 children. He also shares 8 plums between them. How many pieces of fruit will each child get altogether?

(____ ÷ ____) + (____ ÷ ____) = ____

Grandma shares a bag of 32 candies between 4 children. She then adds 2 of her homemade candies to each child's pile. How many candies will each child receive?

(____ ÷ ____) + ____ = ____

Greater, Less Than, or Equal

Remember that < means **less than** and that > means **greater than**.

Write <, >, or = in each box.

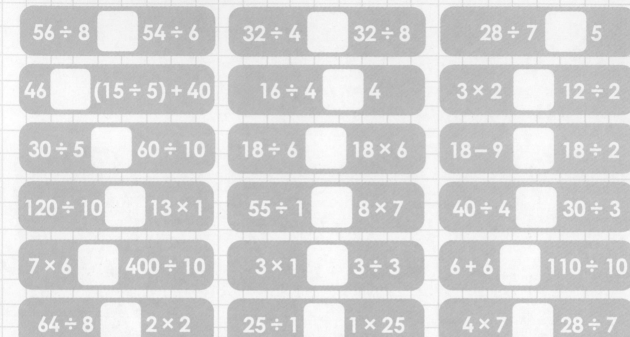

56 ÷ 8 ☐ 54 ÷ 6	32 ÷ 4 ☐ 32 ÷ 8	28 ÷ 7 ☐ 5
46 ☐ (15 ÷ 5) + 40	16 ÷ 4 ☐ 4	3 × 2 ☐ 12 ÷ 2
30 ÷ 5 ☐ 60 ÷ 10	18 ÷ 6 ☐ 18 × 6	18 − 9 ☐ 18 ÷ 2
120 ÷ 10 ☐ 13 × 1	55 ÷ 1 ☐ 8 × 7	40 ÷ 4 ☐ 30 ÷ 3
7 × 6 ☐ 400 ÷ 10	3 × 1 ☐ 3 ÷ 3	6 + 6 ☐ 110 ÷ 10
64 ÷ 8 ☐ 2 × 2	25 ÷ 1 ☐ 1 × 25	4 × 7 ☐ 28 ÷ 7
12 − 6 − 6 ☐ 6 ÷ 6	2 × 6 ☐ (27 ÷ 3) − 2	(35 ÷ 7) + 1 ☐ 5

Solve the problems. Show your work.

A bag of 3 model planes costs $24. Individually, the same model planes cost $9. Is it cheaper to buy 3 planes individually or in a bag?

_____

At Value Mart, a pack of 7 pens cost $14. At Bargain Mart, you can buy 4 of the same pens for $12. Which store offers the cheapest price per pen?

_____

Dividends and Divisors

Remember, you can use your times-table and place-value knowledge to figure out the answers.

Fill in the missing dividends and divisors.

49 ÷ ___ = 7	___ ÷ 4 = 8	35 ÷ ___ = 5	___ ÷ 1 = 43
___ ÷ 6 = 8	40 ÷ ___ = 4	460 ÷ ___ = 46	63 ÷ ___ = 7
9 ÷ ___ = 9	___ ÷ 2 = 8	56 ÷ ___ = 8	___ ÷ 6 = 4
___ ÷ 7 = 3	72 ÷ ___ = 8	___ ÷ 10 = 8	1 ÷ ___ = 1
16 ÷ ___ = 4	___ ÷ 3 = 9	100 ÷ ___ = 10	28 ÷ ___ = 7
9 ÷ ___ = 3	___ ÷ 4 = 5	360 ÷ ___ = 36	62 ÷ ___ = 62

Write equations to solve the word problems. Circle the answers.

Jenny has $30 to spend on rabbit food. Each bag of food costs $6. How many bags can she afford?

$30 ÷ $ [ ] = [ ]

A farmer has 90 bales of hay to share evenly among 6 fields of cattle. How many bales will each field get?

⟌90

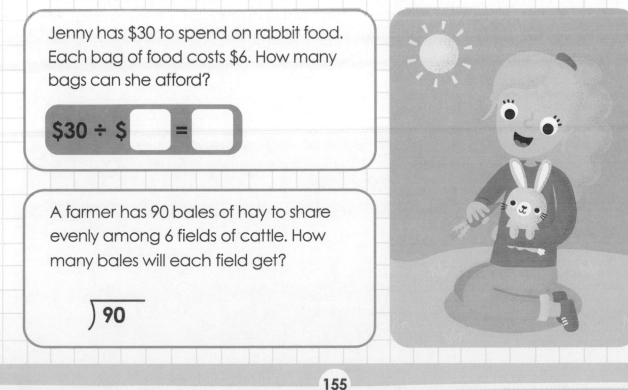

Word Problems

Underlining the number facts can help solve word problems. In the first question, underline 78 party decorations and bags of 6.

Solve the problems. Show your work.

A storekeeper buys a bulk lot of 78 party decorations. She wants to sell them in bags of 6. How many bags will she fill?

$6\overline{)78}$

A farmer wants to divide a crate of 84 eggs into boxes of 6. How many boxes of eggs will he have to sell?

There are 26 shoes in the Miller children's closet. How many pairs of shoes are there?

Dad divides 9 shirts into 3 ironing piles. He then adds two pairs of pants to each pile. How many pieces of clothing are in each pile?

(___ ÷ ___) + ___ = ___

A sports coach divides 54 tennis balls into baskets of 6 balls each. A dog then steals one of the baskets. How many baskets does she have left?

(___ ÷ ___) − ___ = ___

Mr. Appleton asks a bank teller to change a $100 bill into $5 bills. How many $5 bills will he be given?

Fact Families

You only need to know the answer to one problem to solve all four problems in any fact family set.

Complete the fact families. In the last row, create your own fact families.

$50 \times 2 = 100$	$3 \times 20 = 60$	$20 \times 4 = 80$
$2 \times 50 = 100$	___ × ___ = ___	___ × ___ = ___
$100 \div 2 = 50$	___ ÷ ___ = ___	___ ÷ ___ = ___
$100 \div 50 = 2$	___ ÷ ___ = ___	___ ÷ ___ = ___

$20 \times 5 = 100$	$2 \times 25 = 50$	$40 \times 2 = 80$
___ × ___ = ___	___ × ___ = ___	___ × ___ = ___
___ ÷ ___ = ___	___ ÷ ___ = ___	___ ÷ ___ = ___
___ ÷ ___ = ___	___ ÷ ___ = ___	___ ÷ ___ = ___

$25 \times 3 = 75$	$10 \times 200 = 2,000$	$24 \times 38 = 912$
___ × ___ = ___	___ × ___ = ___	___ × ___ = ___
___ ÷ ___ = ___	___ ÷ ___ = ___	___ ÷ ___ = ___
___ ÷ ___ = ___	___ ÷ ___ = ___	___ ÷ ___ = ___

___ × ___ = ___	___ × ___ = ___
___ × ___ = ___	___ × ___ = ___
___ ÷ ___ = ___	___ ÷ ___ = ___
___ ÷ ___ = ___	___ ÷ ___ = ___

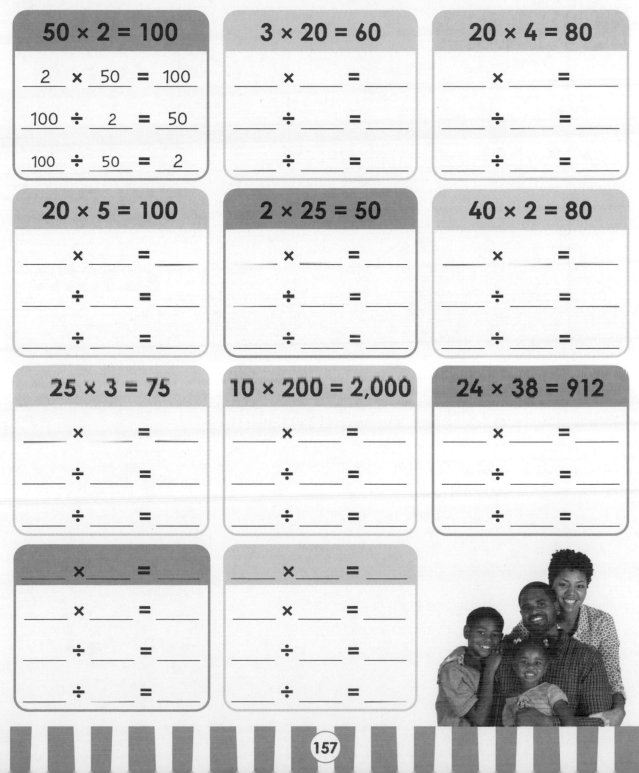

Halves

When you divide a number or anything else into **2 equal pieces**, you divide it in half. The one-half symbol, $\frac{1}{2}$, means 1 of 2 equal parts.

Sticker $\frac{1}{2}$ of each shape **blue** and the other $\frac{1}{2}$ **orange**.

How many halves make one whole shape? ___

Check the shapes where exactly $\frac{1}{2}$ is shaded.

☐   ☐   ☐   ☐

Divide by two to solve the word problems.

Mom has 6 candies. She tells Harper and Ethan that they can have $\frac{1}{2}$ each. How many candies will each child get?

6 ÷ ___ **=** ___

Harry takes 8 jelly beans from a jar and gives half of them to a friend. How many jelly beans will each child get?

___ **÷ 2 =** ___

Thirds

When you divide a number or anything else into **3 equal pieces**, you divide it into thirds. The one-third symbol, $\frac{1}{3}$, means 1 of 3 equal parts.

Color $\frac{1}{3}$ of each shape **red**, $\frac{1}{3}$ green, and $\frac{1}{3}$ yellow.

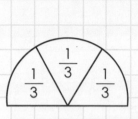

$\frac{1}{3}$ $\frac{1}{3}$ $\frac{1}{3}$

$\frac{1}{3}$ $\frac{1}{3}$ $\frac{1}{3}$ $\frac{1}{3}$

$\frac{1}{3}$ $\frac{1}{3}$ $\frac{1}{3}$

How many thirds make one whole shape? ___

Check the shapes where exactly $\frac{1}{3}$ is shaded.

☐   ☐   ☐   ☐

Divide by three to solve the word problems.

Dad shares $18 between 3 children. If he gives them each $\frac{1}{3}$, how much will each child get?

$18 ÷ ___ = $ ___

Lara shares 9 cookies among two friends and herself. If they each get $\frac{1}{3}$, how many cookies will each child get?

___ ÷ 3 = ___

Quarters

When you divide a number or anything else into **4 equal pieces**, you divide it into fourths, or quarters. The one-fourth symbol, $\frac{1}{4}$, means 1 of 4 equal parts.

Shade $\frac{1}{4}$ of each shape **blue**, $\frac{1}{4}$ **purple**, $\frac{1}{4}$ **orange**, and the last $\frac{1}{4}$ **green**.

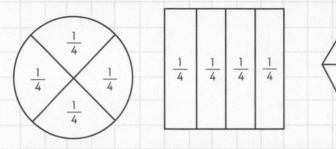

How many quarters make one whole shape? ___

Check the shapes where exactly $\frac{1}{4}$ is shaded.

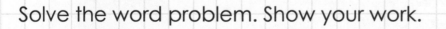

Solve the word problem. Show your work.

One dollar is 100 cents. A quarter coin is 25 cents. How many quarters do you need to make a dollar? (There's a hint in the word *quarter*.)

_____

_____

_____

Parts of a Whole

A fraction's **lower number** tells you how many parts make up the whole.
The **top number** tells you how many of those parts we're focusing on.

Under the line, write the total number of parts in each shape.
Above the line, write the **number of parts** that are shaded.

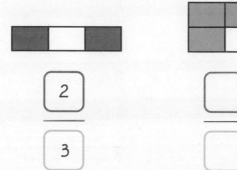  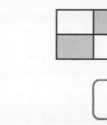 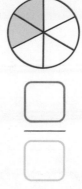

2
—
3

☐
—
☐

☐
—
☐

☐
—
☐

Shade the boxes to match the fractions.

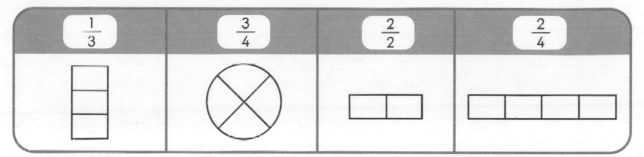

| $\frac{1}{3}$ | $\frac{3}{4}$ | $\frac{2}{2}$ | $\frac{2}{4}$ |

Write the words as number fractions.

two-thirds   **four-fifths**   **three-sixths**

2
—
3

☐
—
☐

☐
—
☐

five-eighths   **six-tenths**   **one-ninth**

☐
—
☐

☐
—
☐

☐
—
☐

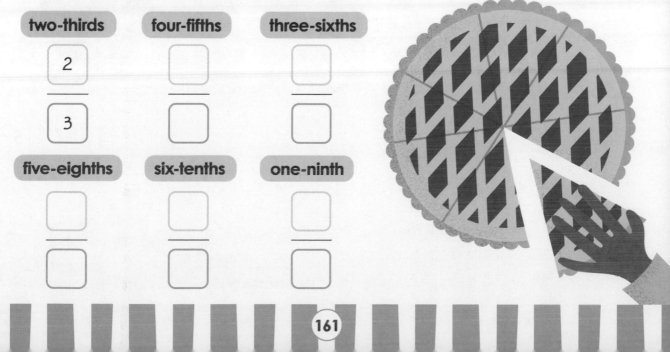

Parts of a Group

The lower number in a fraction is called the **denominator**.
The top number is called the **numerator**.

Write the fraction of each group that is shaded.

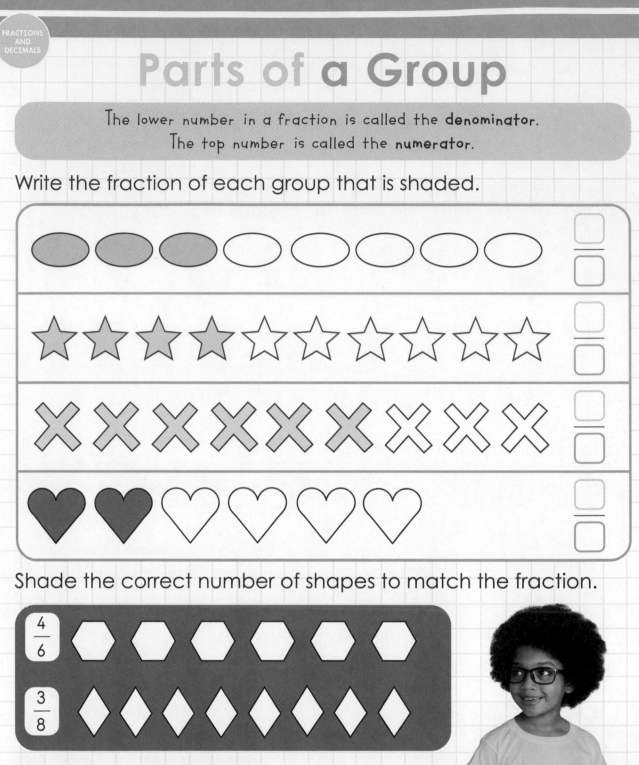

Shade the correct number of shapes to match the fraction.

$\frac{4}{6}$

$\frac{3}{8}$

Solve the word problem.

There are 7 model animals in a set. Annie has 4 of them. What fraction of the whole set has she collected?

Fractions and Division

In **division**, we divide a number into equal-sized smaller numbers.
With **fractions**, we divide 1 whole into equal-sized pieces smaller than 1.

Solve the problems, and then shade the correct fraction.

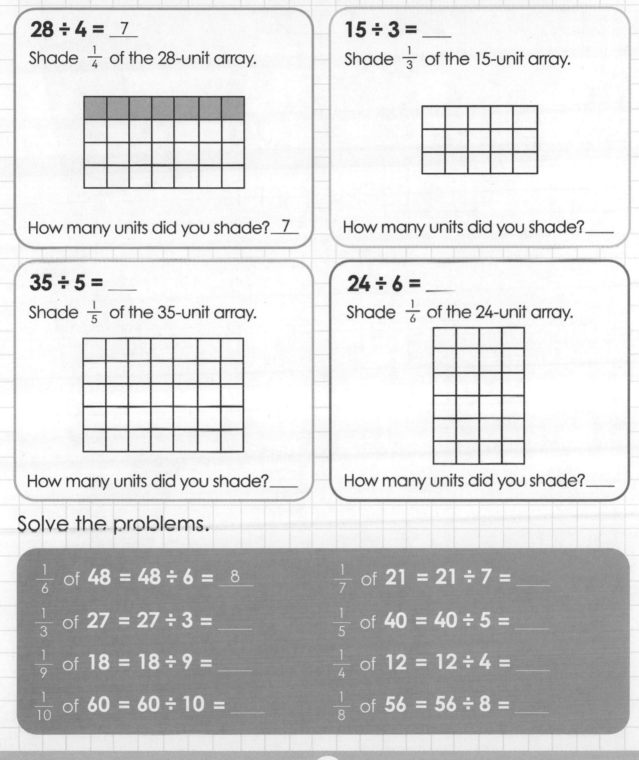

28 ÷ 4 = _7_
Shade $\frac{1}{4}$ of the 28-unit array.

How many units did you shade?_7_

15 ÷ 3 = ___
Shade $\frac{1}{3}$ of the 15-unit array.

How many units did you shade?___

35 ÷ 5 = ___
Shade $\frac{1}{5}$ of the 35-unit array.

How many units did you shade?___

24 ÷ 6 = ___
Shade $\frac{1}{6}$ of the 24-unit array.

How many units did you shade?___

Solve the problems.

$\frac{1}{6}$ of **48 = 48 ÷ 6 =** _8_

$\frac{1}{3}$ of **27 = 27 ÷ 3 =** ___

$\frac{1}{9}$ of **18 = 18 ÷ 9 =** ___

$\frac{1}{10}$ of **60 = 60 ÷ 10 =** ___

$\frac{1}{7}$ of **21 = 21 ÷ 7 =** ___

$\frac{1}{5}$ of **40 = 40 ÷ 5 =** ___

$\frac{1}{4}$ of **12 = 12 ÷ 4 =** ___

$\frac{1}{8}$ of **56 = 56 ÷ 8 =** ___

Add Fractions

It's easy to add fractions with the **same denominator**.
Just add the numerators.

Use the diagrams to help you add the fractions.

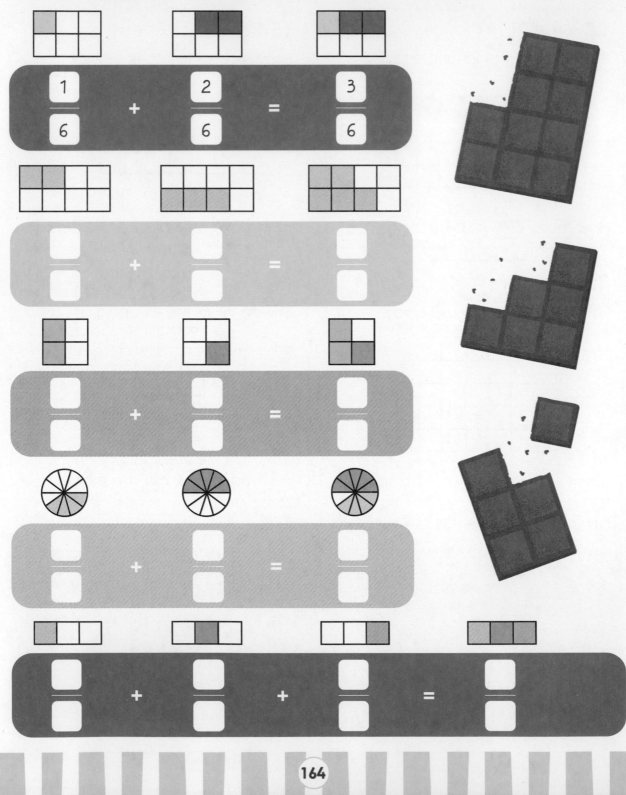

$$\frac{1}{6} + \frac{2}{6} = \frac{3}{6}$$

Add Fractions

If you find adding fractions hard, **draw diagrams** like the ones below to help you picture what's happening.

Shade the boxes to help you add the fractions.

$$\frac{1}{4} + \frac{1}{4} = \boxed{}$$

$$\frac{2}{6} + \frac{3}{6} = \boxed{}$$

Add the fractions.

$$\frac{1}{5} + \frac{3}{5} = \boxed{}$$ $$\frac{3}{7} + \frac{2}{7} = \boxed{}$$ $$\frac{1}{2} + \frac{1}{2} = \boxed{}$$

$$\frac{4}{8} + \frac{2}{8} = \boxed{}$$ $$\frac{1}{9} + \frac{1}{9} = \boxed{}$$ $$\frac{4}{10} + \frac{4}{10} = \boxed{}$$

$$\frac{2}{20} + \frac{11}{20} = \boxed{}$$ $$\frac{5}{12} + \frac{6}{12} = \boxed{}$$ $$\frac{1}{3} + \frac{1}{3} = \boxed{}$$

$$\frac{8}{17} + \frac{4}{17} = \boxed{}$$ $$\frac{7}{30} + \frac{20}{30} = \boxed{}$$ $$\frac{3}{100} + \frac{94}{100} = \boxed{}$$

Subtract Fractions

To subtract fractions with the **same denominator**, take the second numerator away from the first. The denominator stays the same.

Cross out fractions of the diagrams to solve the problems.

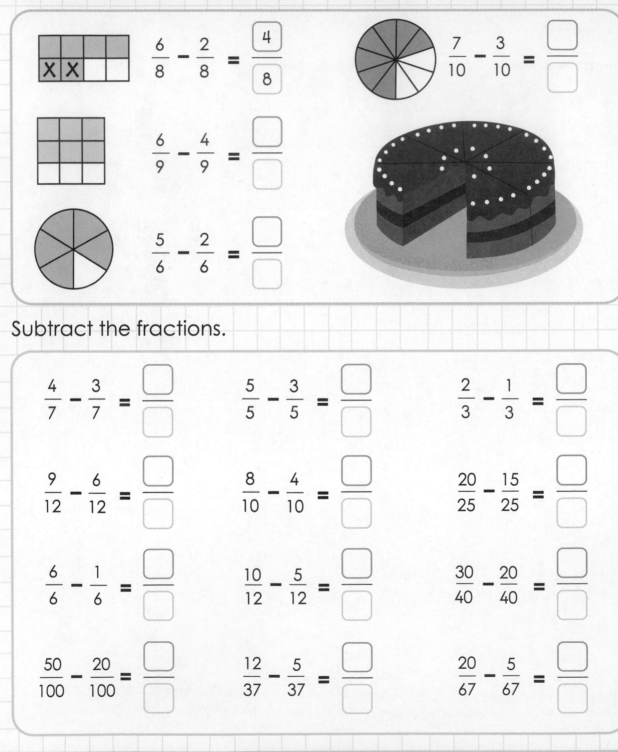

$\frac{6}{8} - \frac{2}{8} = \frac{4}{8}$

$\frac{7}{10} - \frac{3}{10} = \frac{\square}{\square}$

$\frac{6}{9} - \frac{4}{9} = \frac{\square}{\square}$

$\frac{5}{6} - \frac{2}{6} = \frac{\square}{\square}$

Subtract the fractions.

$\frac{4}{7} - \frac{3}{7} = \frac{\square}{\square}$

$\frac{5}{5} - \frac{3}{5} = \frac{\square}{\square}$

$\frac{2}{3} - \frac{1}{3} = \frac{\square}{\square}$

$\frac{9}{12} - \frac{6}{12} = \frac{\square}{\square}$

$\frac{8}{10} - \frac{4}{10} = \frac{\square}{\square}$

$\frac{20}{25} - \frac{15}{25} = \frac{\square}{\square}$

$\frac{6}{6} - \frac{1}{6} = \frac{\square}{\square}$

$\frac{10}{12} - \frac{5}{12} = \frac{\square}{\square}$

$\frac{30}{40} - \frac{20}{40} = \frac{\square}{\square}$

$\frac{50}{100} - \frac{20}{100} = \frac{\square}{\square}$

$\frac{12}{37} - \frac{5}{37} = \frac{\square}{\square}$

$\frac{20}{67} - \frac{5}{67} = \frac{\square}{\square}$

Equivalent Fractions

Some fractions stand for **the same amount**. For example, if you eat $\frac{2}{4}$ of a pizza, altogether you've eaten $\frac{1}{2}$ the pizza. $\frac{2}{4} = \frac{1}{2}$

Write the fraction of each shape that is shaded. Circle the equivalent fractions in each group.

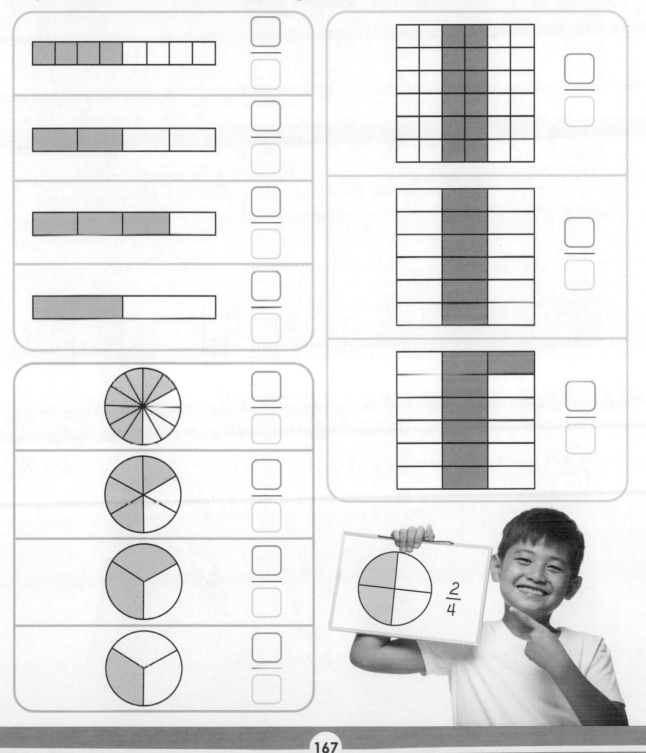

FRACTIONS AND DECIMALS

Greater, Less Than, or Equal

Remember that < means **less than** and that > means **greater than**.

Write <, >, or = in each box. Use the diagrams to help you.

$\dfrac{3}{6}$ ☐ $\dfrac{4}{6}$

$\dfrac{5}{8}$ ☐ $\dfrac{1}{2}$

$\dfrac{2}{5}$ ☐ $\dfrac{3}{5}$

$\dfrac{1}{2}$ ☐ $\dfrac{2}{4}$

$\dfrac{7}{9}$ ☐ $\dfrac{2}{3}$

$\dfrac{4}{8}$ ☐ $\dfrac{2}{4}$

$\dfrac{7}{10}$ ☐ $\dfrac{4}{5}$

$\dfrac{4}{6}$ ☐ $\dfrac{2}{3}$

Picture Fractions

Fraction diagrams help you compare different-sized fractions of the same shape.

Finish coloring the fraction diagram.

1

| $\frac{1}{2}$ | $\frac{1}{2}$ |

| $\frac{1}{3}$ | $\frac{1}{3}$ | $\frac{1}{3}$ |

| $\frac{1}{4}$ | $\frac{1}{4}$ | $\frac{1}{4}$ | $\frac{1}{4}$ |

| $\frac{1}{5}$ | $\frac{1}{5}$ | $\frac{1}{5}$ | $\frac{1}{5}$ | $\frac{1}{5}$ |

| $\frac{1}{6}$ | $\frac{1}{6}$ | $\frac{1}{6}$ | $\frac{1}{6}$ | $\frac{1}{6}$ | $\frac{1}{6}$ |

| $\frac{1}{7}$ | $\frac{1}{7}$ | $\frac{1}{7}$ | $\frac{1}{7}$ | $\frac{1}{7}$ | $\frac{1}{7}$ | $\frac{1}{7}$ |

| $\frac{1}{8}$ | $\frac{1}{8}$ | $\frac{1}{8}$ | $\frac{1}{8}$ | $\frac{1}{8}$ | $\frac{1}{8}$ | $\frac{1}{8}$ | $\frac{1}{8}$ |

| $\frac{1}{9}$ | $\frac{1}{9}$ | $\frac{1}{9}$ | $\frac{1}{9}$ | $\frac{1}{9}$ | $\frac{1}{9}$ | $\frac{1}{9}$ | $\frac{1}{9}$ | $\frac{1}{9}$ |

| $\frac{1}{10}$ | $\frac{1}{10}$ | $\frac{1}{10}$ | $\frac{1}{10}$ | $\frac{1}{10}$ | $\frac{1}{10}$ | $\frac{1}{10}$ | $\frac{1}{10}$ | $\frac{1}{10}$ | $\frac{1}{10}$ |

Use the diagram to help you solve the word problems.

Hailey ate $\frac{1}{2}$ of a pizza, and Luke ate $\frac{1}{3}$ of it. Who had the most pizza?

_____

By dinnertime, Riley had done $\frac{3}{6}$ of her homework, and her twin, Noah, had done $\frac{2}{3}$ of his. Who had done more of their homework?

_____

Zoe said that she'd eaten $\frac{5}{10}$ of the candy in the box.
Can you name a simpler fraction that means the same as $\frac{5}{10}$?

_____

Improper Fractions

We can write a **whole number** as a fraction. $8 = \frac{8}{1}$ and $14 = \frac{14}{1}$
An **improper fraction** has a higher numerator than denominator.
We can convert it to a mixed number. $\frac{7}{3} = 2\frac{1}{3}$

Convert the whole numbers to fractions.

$5 = \dfrac{5}{1}$ $9 = \underline{\hspace{1cm}}$ $12 = \underline{\hspace{1cm}}$ $37 = \underline{\hspace{1cm}}$

$50 = \underline{\hspace{1cm}}$ $256 = \underline{\hspace{1cm}}$ $777 = \underline{\hspace{1cm}}$ $1,000 = \underline{\hspace{1cm}}$

Rewrite the improper fractions as mixed numbers.

$\dfrac{9}{4} = 2\frac{1}{4}$

$\dfrac{8}{6} = \underline{\hspace{1cm}}$

$\dfrac{3}{2} = \underline{\hspace{1cm}}$

$\dfrac{16}{6} = \underline{\hspace{1cm}}$

$\dfrac{7}{3} = \underline{\hspace{1cm}}$

$\dfrac{21}{12} = \underline{\hspace{1cm}}$

$\dfrac{12}{5} = \underline{\hspace{1cm}}$

$\dfrac{20}{8} = \underline{\hspace{1cm}}$

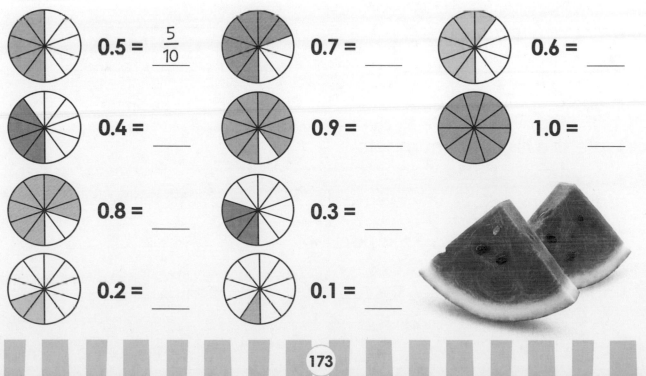

Fractions and Decimals

Decimal numbers are a way of writing tenths, hundredths, and thousandths without using fractions. The fraction $\frac{3}{10}$ is written as 0.3.

Convert the fractions to decimals. Put a zero and a point (or dot) in front of the number of tenths.

$\frac{3}{10}$ = __0.3__

$\frac{7}{10}$ = __0.7__

$\frac{2}{10}$ = _____

$\frac{5}{10}$ = _____

$\frac{4}{10}$ = _____

$\frac{9}{10}$ = _____

$\frac{1}{10}$ = _____

$\frac{10}{10}$ = _____

Convert the decimals to fractions.

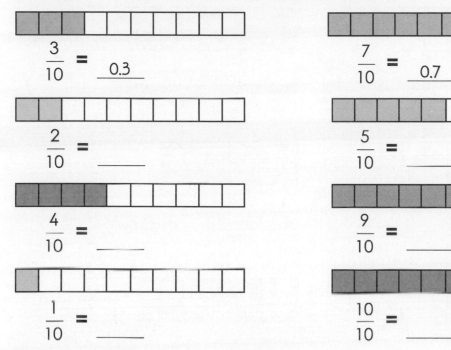

0.5 = $\frac{5}{10}$

0.7 = _____

0.6 = _____

0.4 = _____

0.9 = _____

1.0 = _____

0.8 = _____

0.3 = _____

0.2 = _____

0.1 = _____

Tenths

People **describe decimals** in different ways. The decimal 0.2 is best described as **two-tenths**, but you might also hear people say **zero point two**.

Write a fraction and decimal for the shaded part of each rectangle.

fraction: $\frac{5}{10}$ decimal: 0.5

fraction: _____   decimal: _____

fraction: _____   decimal: _____

fraction: _____   decimal: _____

fraction: _____   decimal: _____

fraction: _____   decimal: _____

fraction: _____   decimal: _____

fraction: _____   decimal: _____

Write the decimal numbers.

five-tenths _____   seven-tenths _____   nine-tenths _____

zero point six _____   zero point two _____ $\frac{4}{10}$ _____

$\frac{1}{10}$ _____ $\frac{8}{10}$ _____ $\frac{10}{10}$ _____

Mixed Numbers

If we have 0.5 of a pizza, we'd often say we have **half a pizza**. If we have 1.5 pizzas, we say we have **one-and-a-half pizzas**.

Write mixed-number fractions and decimals to describe the shaded regions.

fraction: 2 $\frac{4}{10}$ decimal: 2.4

fraction: _____   decimal: _____

fraction: _____   decimal: _____

fraction: _____   decimal: _____

fraction: _____   decimal: _____

fraction: _____   decimal: _____

Covert the mixed-number fractions to decimals.

5 $\frac{2}{10}$ = 5.2	7 $\frac{1}{10}$ = _____	9 $\frac{9}{10}$ = _____
12 $\frac{6}{10}$ = _____	20 $\frac{3}{10}$ = _____	1 $\frac{1}{10}$ = _____
32 $\frac{8}{10}$ = _____	102 $\frac{5}{10}$ = _____	528 $\frac{4}{10}$ = _____

Hundredths

If you break one whole into 100 same-size pieces, each piece is called a **hundredth**. Ten hundredths create one tenth.

Write = or ≠ to say whether the shaded tenths and hundredths are equal or not equal.

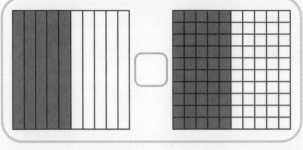   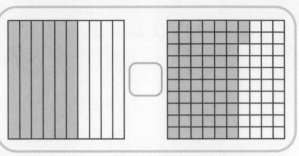

Write a fraction and a decimal to describe each shaded part. Then complete the sentences.

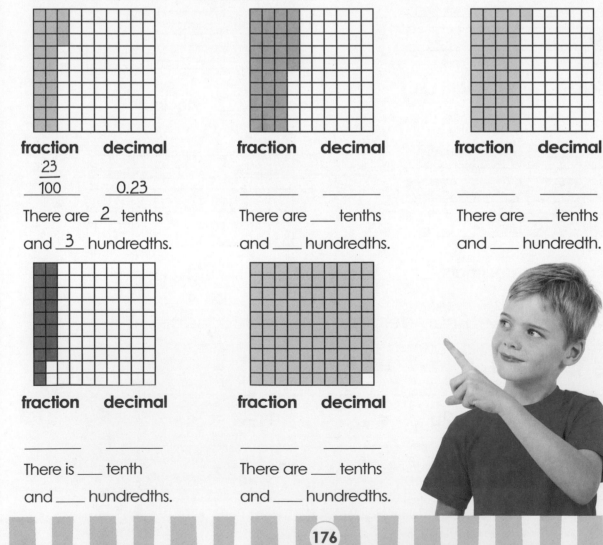

fraction   decimal

$\dfrac{23}{100}$ 0.23

There are _2_ tenths
and _3_ hundredths.

fraction   decimal

_____   _____

There are ___ tenths
and ___ hundredths.

fraction   decimal

_____   _____

There are ___ tenths
and ___ hundredth.

fraction   decimal

_____   _____

There is ___ tenth
and ___ hundredths.

fraction   decimal

_____   _____

There are ___ tenths
and ___ hundredths.

Hundredths

In a place-value chart, each position is **ten times smaller** than the position to its left. A hundredth is ten times smaller than a tenth.

Write the digits that make up each number under the correct columns in the place-value chart. Then add four more numbers to the chart.

	hundreds	tens	ones	•	tenths	hundredths
527.08	5	2	7	•	0	8
6.20			6	•	2	0
367.12				•		
808.44				•		
67.28				•		
8.24				•		
300.30				•		
69.07				•		
636.63				•		
238.92				•		
36.73				•		
1.10				•		
562.26				•		
999.09				•		
				•		
				•		
				•		
				•		

Decimal Currency

One dollar is one unit of money. **Cents** are worth less than a dollar.
They are **hundredths** of a dollar.

Write the money values as decimal numbers.

Twenty-five dollars and thirty-four cents $25.34

Six dollars and four cents $6.04

Thirty-six dollars and fifty-seven cents   _____

Twelve dollars and twenty-seven cents   _____

Fifty-nine dollars and forty cents   _____

Ten dollars and six cents   _____

Write the prices in order from cheapest to most expensive.

$12.45	$12.50	$12.48	_____	_____	_____
$4.20	$4.00	$4.02	_____	_____	_____
$6.00	$5.99	$6.99	_____	_____	_____
$72.56	$73.56	$72.57	_____	_____	_____
$56.99	$56.00	$55.99	_____	_____	_____

$6.00

$12.45

$73.56

Word Problems

When solving word problems, it is often helpful to **write equations** or to **draw diagrams**. This can help you see the problem more clearly.

Solve the problems. Show your work or give reasons for your answer.

Sophy opened a pack of 10 cookies. She ate $\frac{2}{10}$ of the cookies and gave $\frac{1}{10}$ to her brother. How many tenths were left?

_____

Eve said she'd washed $\frac{1}{2}$ of the dishes. Ethan said he'd washed $\frac{2}{4}$ of them. Who, if either, had washed the most dishes?

_____

Caden bought a book costing $5.99. Aria bought the same book in another store. She paid $6.00. Who paid more?

_____

Harper's dad gave her 100 one-penny coins. How many dollars were they worth?

_____

Leo spelled 8 out of 10 words correctly in his spelling quiz. Write this score as a fraction and as a decimal.

_____

Leah got 82 questions out of 100 correct in her math test. Write this score as a fraction and as a decimal.

_____

Convert Units

We can break units of measurement into smaller units. For example, we can record a box's length as **1 meter (m)** or **100 centimeters (cm)**.

Use the chart to solve the problems.

Length	Volume	Weight
10 millimeters (mm) = 1 centimeter (cm)	10 milliliters (ml) = 1 centiliter (cl)	10 milligrams (mg) = 1 centigram (cg)
100 centimeters (cm) = 1 meter (m)	100 centiliters (cl) = 1 liter (l)	100 centigrams (cg) = 1 gram (g)
1,000 meters (m) = 1 kilometer (km)	1,000 liters (l) = 1 kiloliter (kl)	1,000 grams (g) = 1 kilogram (kg)

40 mm = ☐ cm   50 ml = ☐ cl   30 mg = ☐ cg

200 mm = ☐ cm   5,000 m = ☐ km   600 cm = ☐ m

4,000 g = ☐ kg   3,000 cl = ☐ l   2,000 l = ☐ kl

Use the chart to solve the word problems. Show your work.

Zara pours 350 ml of juice into a glass.
How many centiliters did she pour?   _____

Jamie runs 5 km to raise money for an animal shelter.
How many meters did Jamie run?   _____

Finish

5 km

Units of Measurement

We often measure large things in **kilo-** measurements, such as **kilometers**, and small things in **milli-** measurements, such as **milligrams**.

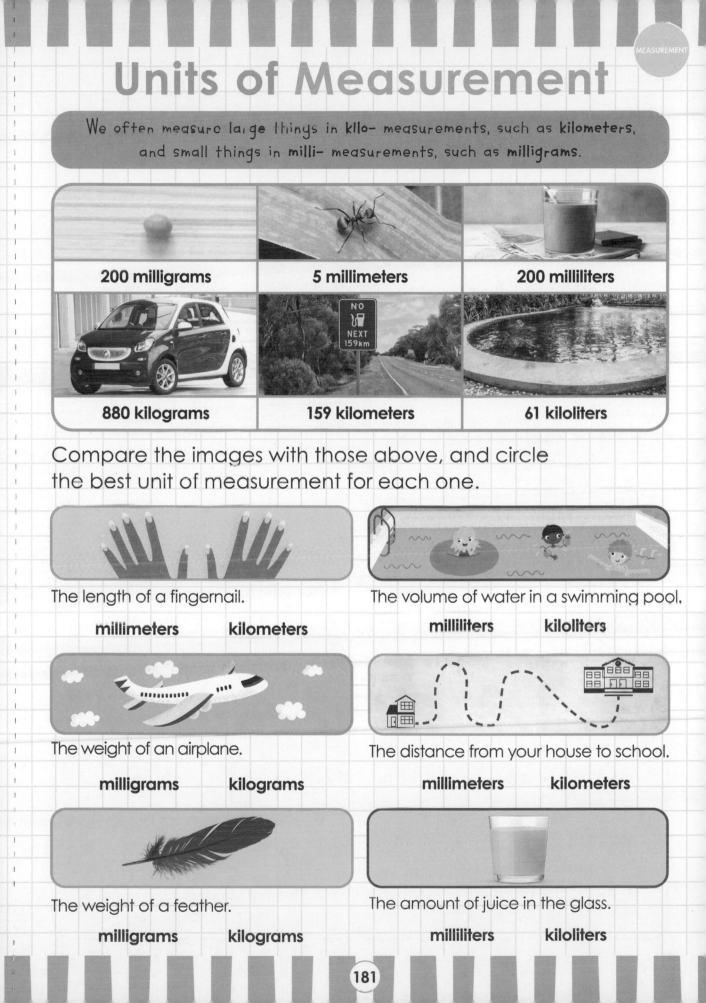

200 milligrams	**5 millimeters**	**200 milliliters**
880 kilograms	**159 kilometers**	**61 kiloliters**

Compare the images with those above, and circle the best unit of measurement for each one.

The length of a fingernail.

millimeters   **kilometers**

The volume of water in a swimming pool.

milliliters   **kiloliters**

The weight of an airplane.

milligrams   **kilograms**

The distance from your house to school.

millimeters   **kilometers**

The weight of a feather.

milligrams   **kilograms**

The amount of juice in the glass.

milliliters   **kiloliters**

Volume and Weight

We can use a measuring cup or beaker to measure **volume**,
and a scale to measure **weight**.

Find the volume. Include the unit of measurement.

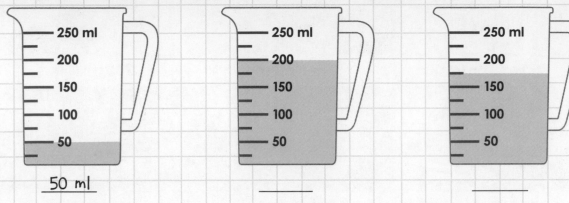

50 ml   _____   _____

Find the weight. Include the unit of measurement.

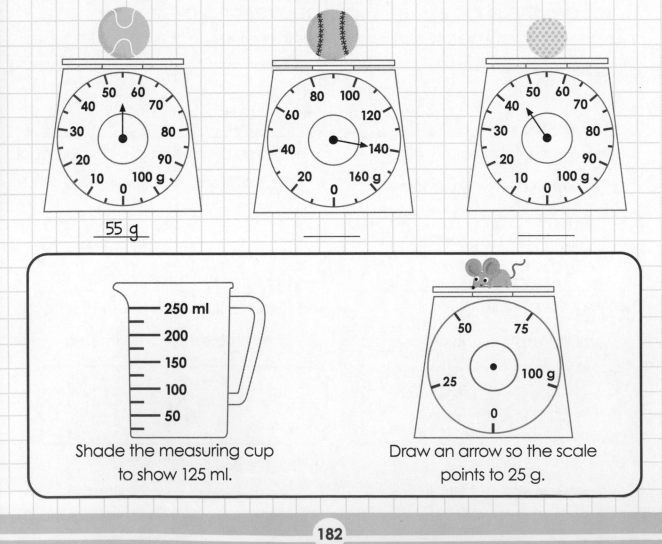

55 g   _____   _____

Shade the measuring cup
to show 125 ml.

Draw an arrow so the scale
points to 25 g.

Make Estimates

> If a scale is not detailed enough to show the measurement we need, we must **estimate** approximately how much we need.

Estimate the volume. Include the unit of measurement.

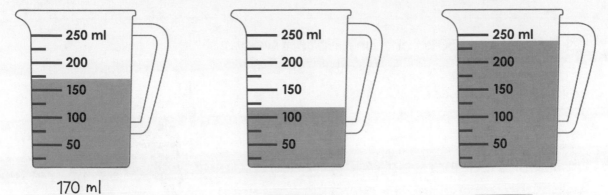

170 ml

_____   _____

Estimate the weight. Include the unit of measurement.

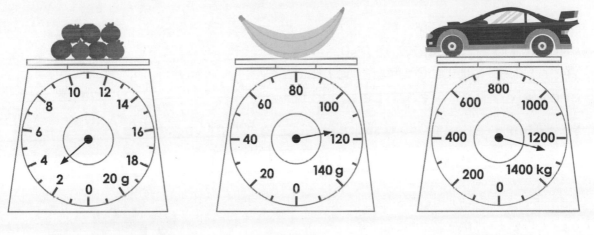

_____   _____   _____

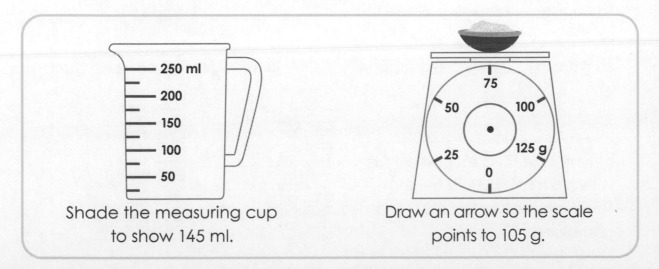

Shade the measuring cup to show 145 ml.

Draw an arrow so the scale points to 105 g.

Word Problems

We can use addition, subtraction, multiplication, and division to solve problems involving measurements.

Solve the problems. Show your work.

If a tiger weighs 250 kg and an elephant weighs 5,540 kg, how much more does the elephant weigh than the tiger? _____ **kg**

Four apples together weigh 400 g. If each apple weighs the same amount, how much does each apple weigh? _____ **g**

Lila is baking cookies for 48 people, but the recipe is for 24 cookies. Help Lila multiply the recipe by 2 to make enough cookies for each person to have one.

90 g flour → _____ **g   50 g sugar →** _____ **g   20 ml vegetable oil →** _____ **ml**

Alex is baking cupcakes for 6 people, but the recipe is for 18 cupcakes. Help Alex divide the recipe by 3 to make 6 cupcakes.

60 g flour → _____ **g   30 g sugar →** _____ **g   15 ml vegetable oil →** _____ **ml**

Oliver fills a beaker with 500 ml of water. He fills a second beaker with 275 ml of oil. How much liquid is in the two beakers combined? _____ **ml**

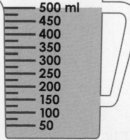

Tangrams

A tangram is a geometric shape composed of seven shapes.
Each tangram is made of five triangles, one square, and one parallelogram.

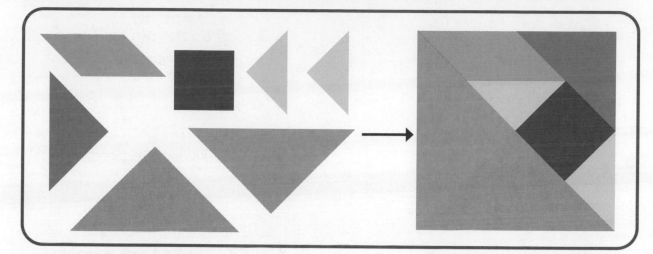

Press out the seven tangram shapes at the back of the book.
Then use them to figure out how to make the shapes below.

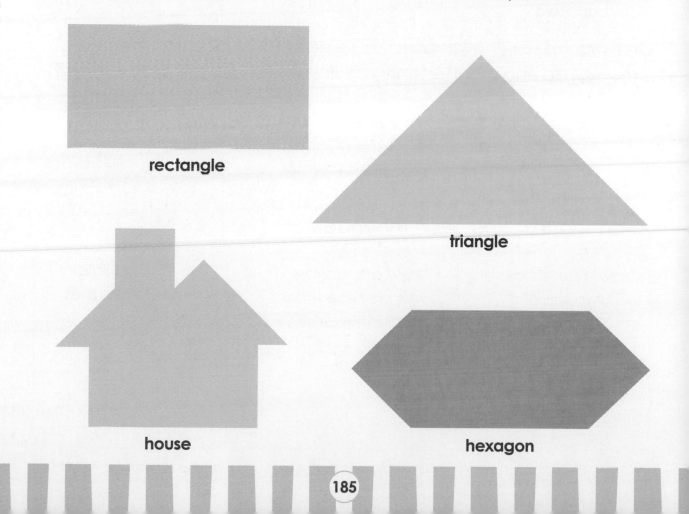

rectangle

triangle

house

hexagon

Quadrilaterals

A **quadrilateral** is a shape with four straight sides.

Match each quadrilateral shape with its best description.

square

Opposite sides are the same length and parallel.

rectangle

Only two sides are parallel.

trapezoid

All sides are the same length, and opposite sides are parallel.

Draw a yellow line connecting each set of parallel lines.
Draw a **red** line connecting the lines that are the same length.

Read the text and draw the shapes.

Draw a quadrilateral with two sets of parallel lines.

Draw a quadrilateral with only one set of parallel lines.

Draw a quadrilateral with no parallel lines.

Picture Graphs

Picture graphs use images to represent data.

Mr. Meyer asked his 25 students to name their favorite ice-cream flavor. He tallied the answers and presented the data on a picture graph. Use the graph to answer the questions.

Students' Favorite Ice-Cream Flavor

Key: Each full symbol represents **two** students.

= strawberry   = chocolate   = vanilla

1 How many more students preferred chocolate to vanilla? _____

2 How many students preferred a flavor other than chocolate? _____

Alice asked her 28 classmates their favorite season.
Use the data she gathered to create a picture graph.

Students' Favorite Season	
winter = 4	
spring = 6	
summer = 12	
fall = 6	

Key: Each full symbol represents **two** students.

 = winter   = spring   = summer   = fall

Bar Graphs

Bar graphs use rectangular bars to show data. Here the **y-axis** is numbered, and the **x-axis** is labeled with categories.

Ms. Cid's class is planning a school trip. Use the graph to answer the questions.

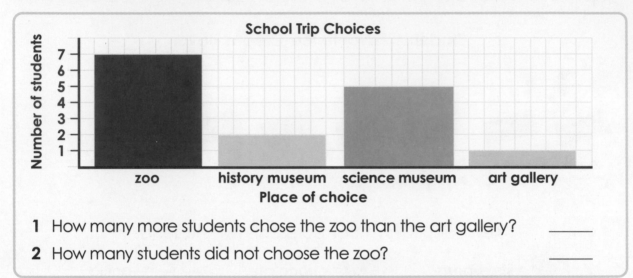

School Trip Choices

1 How many more students chose the zoo than the art gallery? _____

2 How many students did not choose the zoo? _____

Ms. Cid's class voted a second time to choose between the top two options. Use the data below to create a bar graph. Make sure to include a title, and label the x-axis and y-axis.

| zoo = 8 | science museum = 7 |

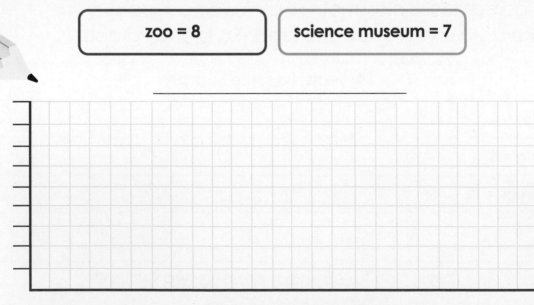

Perimeter

Perimeter is the distance around a 2D shape. To find the perimeter, add the lengths of all the sides.

Find the perimeter of each shape. Include the unit of measurement.

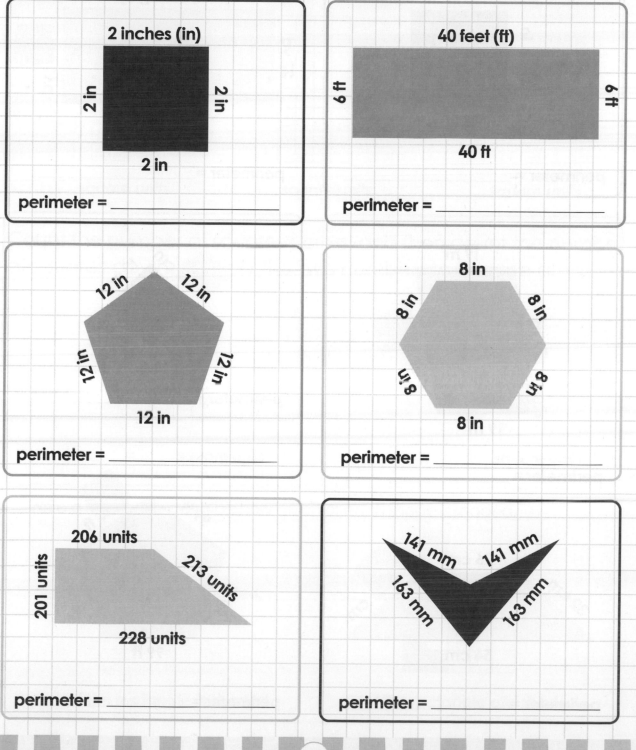

2 inches (in)

2 in

2 in

2 in

perimeter = _____

40 feet (ft)

9 ft

9 ft

40 ft

perimeter = _____

12 in

12 in

12 in

12 in

12 in

perimeter = _____

8 in

8 in

8 in

8 in

8 in

8 in

perimeter = _____

206 units

201 units

213 units

228 units

perimeter = _____

141 mm

141 mm

163 mm

163 mm

perimeter = _____

Area

The short way of writing **square units** is **units²**. The ² means that two numbers have been multiplied together.

Find the area of each shape. For rectangles and parallelograms, use this equation: width (w) × height (h) = area. For squares, use this equation: length of side × itself = area. Show your work.

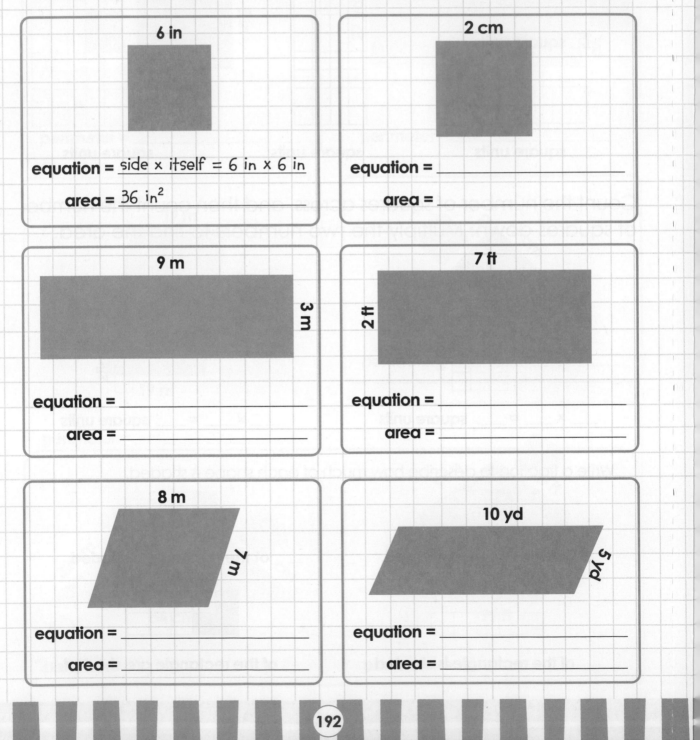

6 in

equation = $\underline{\text{side × itself = 6 in × 6 in}}$

area = $\underline{\text{36 in}^2}$

2 cm

equation = _____

area = _____

9 m

3 m

equation = _____

area = _____

7 ft

2 ft

equation = _____

area = _____

8 m

7 m

equation = _____

area = _____

10 yd

5 yd

equation = _____

area = _____

Add Areas

To find the total area of two shapes that have a side of the same length, add the other two sides together and multiply that number by the number of the side they have in common.

Here are two ways to find the combined area. Show your work and include the unit of measurement.

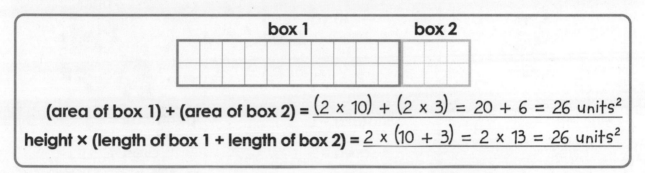

(area of box 1) + (area of box 2) = $(2 \times 10) + (2 \times 3) = 20 + 6 = 26$ units^2

height × (length of box 1 + length of box 2) = $2 \times (10 + 3) = 2 \times 13 = 26$ units^2

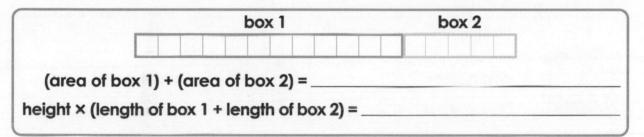

(area of box 1) + (area of box 2) = _____

height × (length of box 1 + length of box 2) = _____

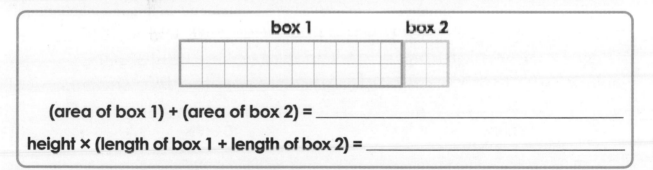

(area of box 1) + (area of box 2) = _____

height × (length of box 1 + length of box 2) = _____

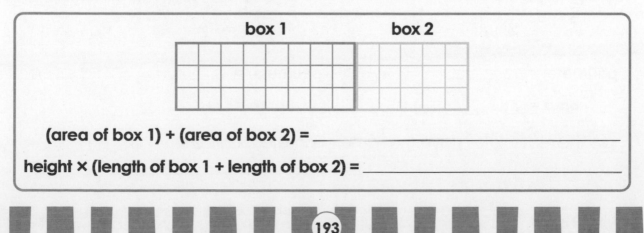

(area of box 1) + (area of box 2) = _____

height × (length of box 1 + length of box 2) = _____

Perimeter and Area

The **perimeter** and **area** of a polygon can be the same number, but the unit of measurement is always different. Remember, for perimeter, we write the units, and for area, we write the units^2.

Find the perimeter and area of each shape.

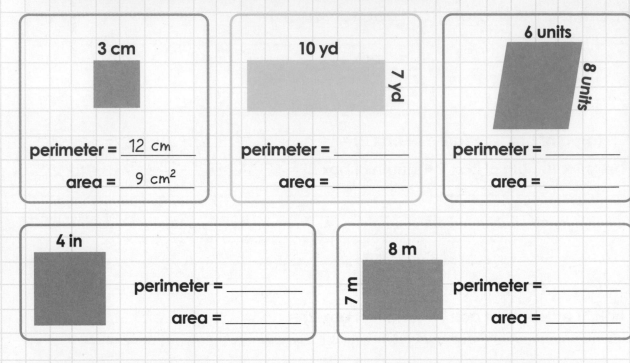

3 cm

perimeter = __12 cm__

area = __9 cm^2__

10 yd

7 yd

perimeter = _____

area = _____

6 units

8 units

perimeter = _____

area = _____

4 in

perimeter = _____

area = _____

8 m

7 m

perimeter = _____

area = _____

Two rectangles can have the same perimeter but different areas, or they might have the same area and different perimeters. Find the perimeter and area of the two shapes.

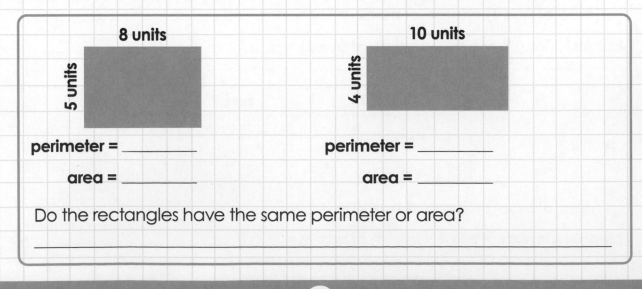

8 units

5 units

perimeter = _____

area = _____

10 units

4 units

perimeter = _____

area = _____

Do the rectangles have the same perimeter or area?

_____

Word Problems

Solve the word problems. Show your work, and include the unit of measurement.

Kevin is hanging a poster with information about the school talent show. The poster measures 8 in by 10 in. What is the area of the poster?

_____

Elsa is making a card for her grandma's birthday and wants to add a border to it. The card measures 5 in by 6 in. What is the perimeter of the card?

_____

Ruth is redecorating her bedroom, which measures 9 ft by 9 ft. What are the area and perimeter of Ruth's room?

_____

Dad is framing a picture. The picture measures 6 cm by 8 cm. What arc the area and perimeter?

_____

Olive is cutting a piece of wrapping paper. The width is 6 cm and the height is 3 cm. She adds 2 cm more to the height. What is the area?

_____

José is planting a rectangular garden. His mom tells him the area is 24 m². If he knows the height is 8 m, what is the width?

_____

Measure Time

We use clocks to tell the time. The short hand shows the hour, and the long hand shows the minute.

Write the times to the nearest minute.

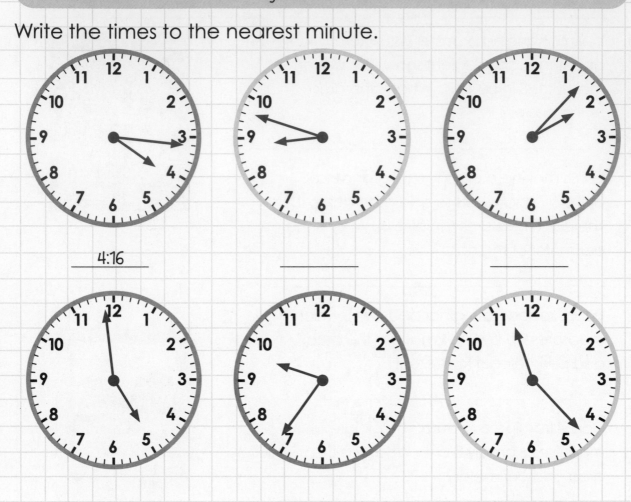

4:16   _____   _____

_____   _____   _____

Draw the times on the clocks.

| 6:54 | 9:39 | 3:12 |

Time Word Problems

Use the number lines to solve the word problems.

1 Emily usually wakes up at 7:05 a.m. Today, she woke up 35 minutes later. What time did Emily wake up?

7:40 a.m.

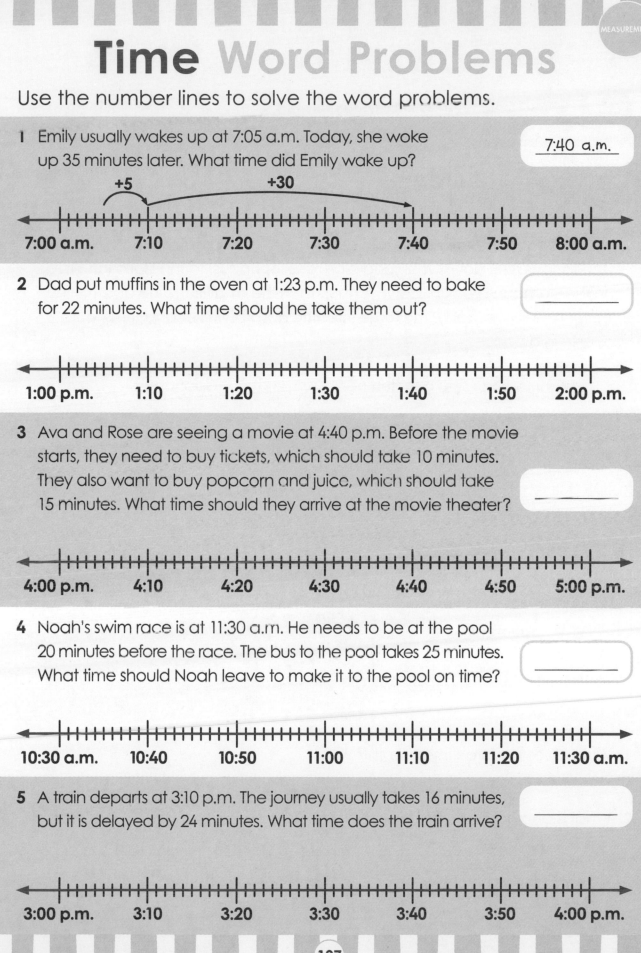

2 Dad put muffins in the oven at 1:23 p.m. They need to bake for 22 minutes. What time should he take them out?

3 Ava and Rose are seeing a movie at 4:40 p.m. Before the movie starts, they need to buy tickets, which should take 10 minutes. They also want to buy popcorn and juice, which should take 15 minutes. What time should they arrive at the movie theater?

4 Noah's swim race is at 11:30 a.m. He needs to be at the pool 20 minutes before the race. The bus to the pool takes 25 minutes. What time should Noah leave to make it to the pool on time?

5 A train departs at 3:10 p.m. The journey usually takes 16 minutes, but it is delayed by 24 minutes. What time does the train arrive?

The Digestive System

Your body's digestive system breaks down the food you eat into nutrients and waste.

Read the text. Then use the word bank to finish labeling the diagram, and answer the questions.

Inside your **mouth**, your teeth and saliva start to break up food. Next, the food travels down your food pipe, or **esophagus**, to the **stomach**. Acid in the stomach breaks it down further. Then the **small intestine** absorbs the nutrients into the body. The **large intestine** absorbs water and turns food waste into poop.

small intestine   large intestine   stomach   esophagus   mouth

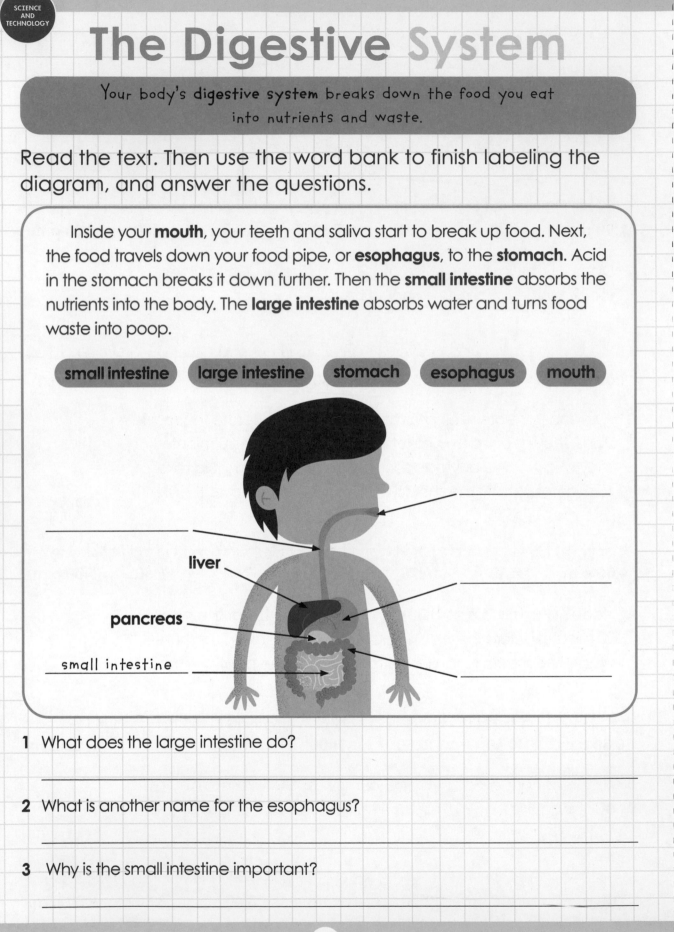

liver

pancreas

small intestine

1 What does the large intestine do?

_____

2 What is another name for the esophagus?

_____

3 Why is the small intestine important?

_____

The Skeletal and Muscular Systems

Your **bones** hold your body in shape and protect your organs.
Your **muscles** pull the bones to make your joints bend and straighten.

Use the diagrams to help you fill in the missing words.

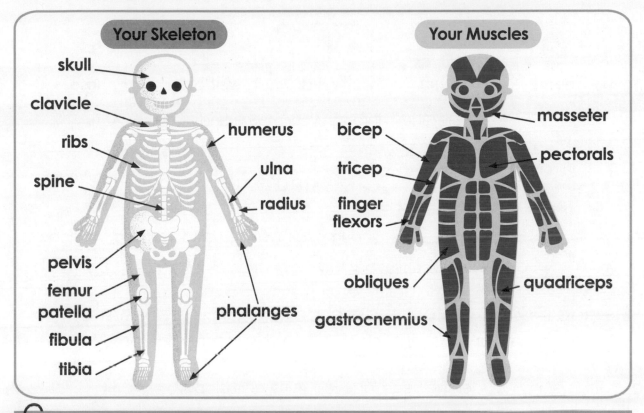

Your Skeleton

skull
clavicle
ribs
spine
humerus
ulna
radius
pelvis
femur
patella
fibula
tibia
phalanges

Your Muscles

masseter
pectorals
bicep
tricep
finger flexors
obliques
gastrocnemius
quadriceps

Your bones make up your s_____ system. Your s_____, or backbone, allows you to sit and stand straight. The s_____ protects your brain, and the r_____ protect your heart and lungs. Arm bones, such as the r_____, and leg bones, such as the f_____, give your limbs shape.

Like your bones, your muscles have names. You use your b_____ and t_____ muscles to bend and straighten your arm. Your thigh muscles are called the q_____, and the chest muscles are called the p_____.

The Circulatory and Respiratory Systems

The **respiratory system** absorbs oxygen and removes carbon dioxide. The **circulatory system** pumps blood around the body. The two systems work together.

Fill in the missing words to complete the sentences.

heart	lungs	veins	windpipe	nose

You breathe in through your mouth and _____.

Air travels down the _____ to the lungs.

Your _____ take in a gas called oxygen and remove carbon dioxide.

The _____ pumps oxygen-rich blood around the body.

Blood circulates back to the heart through the _____.

Decide if each sentence describes the circulatory system or the respiratory system, and circle the correct word.

This system includes the heart, arteries, veins, and blood.

circulatory   respiratory

This system includes the lungs, windpipe, mouth, and nose.

circulatory   respiratory

We breathe in a lot of oxygen and breathe out a lot of carbon dioxide.

circulatory   respiratory

Arteries carry oxygen-rich blood away from the heart to the rest of the body.

circulatory   respiratory

The Brain

Read the text. Then shade the diagram, and answer the questions.

The brain is the control center for the human body. It has many specialized parts.

The **cerebrum** is the largest part of the brain and is responsible for movements you can control, such as dancing or kicking a ball. Your **cerebrum** is also in charge of thinking, solving problems, and remembering.

The **cerebellum** is smaller and sits under the cerebrum at the back of the head. It controls your balance and coordination.

The **brain stem** controls involuntary functions. These are movements your body makes without you thinking about them, such as breathing and the beating of your heart.

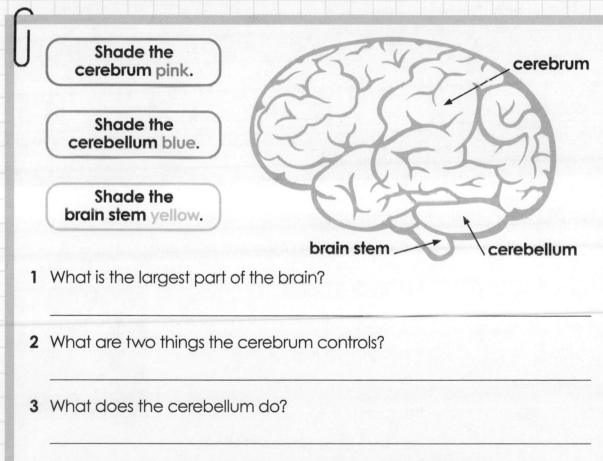

Shade the cerebrum pink.

Shade the cerebellum blue.

Shade the brain stem yellow.

cerebrum

brain stem

cerebellum

1 What is the largest part of the brain?

_____

2 What are two things the cerebrum controls?

_____

3 What does the cerebellum do?

_____

4 Name an involuntary function controlled by the brain stem.

_____

The Solar System

There are **eight planets** in our Solar System, each of which orbits around the Sun.

Use the first letter of each word in the sentence below to help you label the planets.

My **V**ery **E**xcellent **M**other **J**ust **S**ent **U**s **N**achos.

Mercury

Match each planet with its description. You may need to use books or the Internet to find out more.

Earth	the smallest planet
Mars	the planet with the strongest winds
Mercury	the largest planet
Jupiter	the planet where we live
Neptune	the planet that rotates on its side
Saturn	also known as The Red Planet
Uranus	the farthest planet you can see without a telescope
Venus	the hottest planet

Earth

Earth spins, or **rotates**, on its axis, creating day and night. Earth also orbits, or **revolves**, around the Sun. Each orbit creates one Earth year.

Circle the correct word in each sentence.

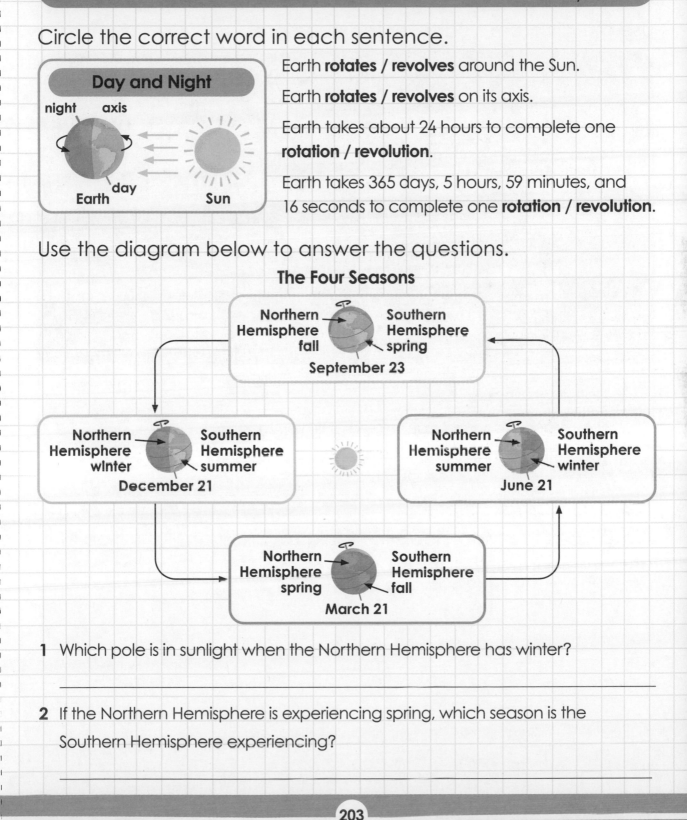

Day and Night

night   axis

day

Earth   Sun

Earth **rotates / revolves** around the Sun.

Earth **rotates / revolves** on its axis.

Earth takes about 24 hours to complete one **rotation / revolution**.

Earth takes 365 days, 5 hours, 59 minutes, and 16 seconds to complete one **rotation / revolution**.

Use the diagram below to answer the questions.

The Four Seasons

Northern Hemisphere fall   Southern Hemisphere spring
September 23

Northern Hemisphere winter   Southern Hemisphere summer
December 21

Northern Hemisphere summer   Southern Hemisphere winter
June 21

Northern Hemisphere spring   Southern Hemisphere fall
March 21

1 Which pole is in sunlight when the Northern Hemisphere has winter?

_____

2 If the Northern Hemisphere is experiencing spring, which season is the Southern Hemisphere experiencing?

_____

The Moon

The **Moon** orbits, or revolves, around Earth about every 27 days. As the Moon moves, different amounts of it are lit by the Sun.

Use the diagram to answer the questions.

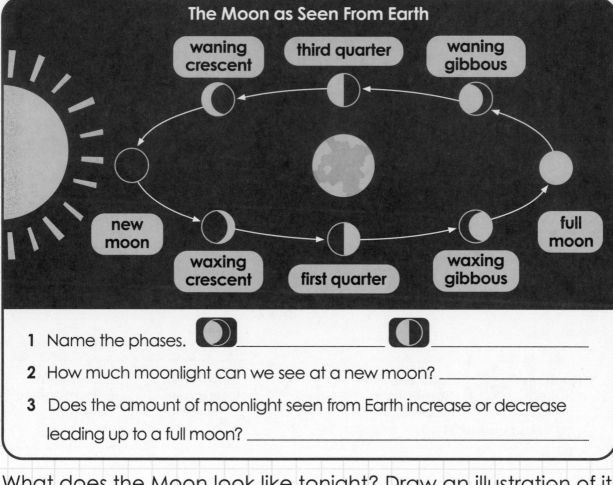

The Moon as Seen From Earth

waning crescent

third quarter

waning gibbous

new moon

full moon

waxing crescent

first quarter

waxing gibbous

1 Name the phases. _____ _____

2 How much moonlight can we see at a new moon? _____

3 Does the amount of moonlight seen from Earth increase or decrease leading up to a full moon? _____

What does the Moon look like tonight? Draw an illustration of it below and label the phase.

Technology in Space

Read the text, and then answer the questions.

NASA has sent five robotic vehicles, called rovers, to Mars to explore the planet. The rovers are called Sojourner, Spirit, Opportunity, Curiosity, and Perseverance. Rovers have wheels and zoom around, collecting data for scientists to study. They investigate the planet's rocks and the chemicals. The most recent rover, Perseverance, landed on Mars in February 2021 to look for signs of past or even present life.

1 What is a rover?

_____

2 How do rovers help scientists?

_____

_____

3 What is Perseverance looking for on Mars?

_____

_____

4 Imagine you're planning a mission to send a rover into space. What planet would you like it to visit, and what might it study?

_____

_____

_____

_____

_____

Animals

Read the text. Then write the animals below in the correct columns, and add five more animals to each side of the chart.

Animals with a backbone are called **vertebrates**. This group includes mammals, such as humans and bears; reptiles, such as crocodiles and snakes; birds; fish; and amphibians, such as frogs.

Invertebrates are animals without a backbone. They include insects, worms, and octopuses. Many invertebrates, such as insects, spiders, and crabs, have a hard outer shell to protect them. Earth is home to many more invertebrates than vertebrates.

jellyfish   rabbit   snail   worm   tiger   lobster   beetle

turtle   butterfly   monkey   parrot   snake

Vertebrates	Invertebrates

Solid, Liquid, or Gas

Everything you see and touch is made of **matter**.
Matter exists in three states: **solid**, **liquid**, and **gas** (vapor).

Complete the chart with items in your home.

Solids	Liquids	Gases
• _a table_	• _shampoo_	• _gas in lightbulbs_
• _____	• _____	• _____
• _____	• _____	• _____
• _____	• _____	• _____

Read the sentences, and then write **melting**, **freezing**, **evaporating**, or **condensing** under each picture.

Solid ice is **melting** into liquid water.   Liquid water is **freezing** into solid ice.

Hot liquid water is **evaporating** into water vapor.

Water vapor is hitting a cold surface and **condensing** into water drops.

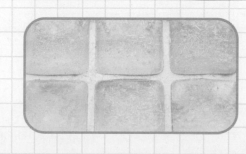

Characteristics

Animals and plants have **characteristics** that help them survive.

Circle the best answer.

How does a polar bear's white fur help it survive?

- It makes the bear soft and fluffy to appeal to tourists.
- The color of its fur blends in with the snow, helping it sneak up on prey.

How does a skunk's smell help it survive?

- The smell attracts other animals.
- The smell scares predators away.

How do the colors on this lizard help it survive?

- The lizard's colors make it more visible to predators.
- The lizard's colors help it blend into its surroundings.

How do sharp spines help a cactus survive?

- They prevent animals from eating the cactus.
- They make the cactus look pretty.

How do bright colors help a poison dart frog survive?

- Predators think it is too cute to eat.
- The bright colors warn predators that the frog is poisonous.

Parts of a Flower

Flowers produce **seeds** that grow into new plants.

Use the first diagram to help you label the second diagram.
Then answer the questions.

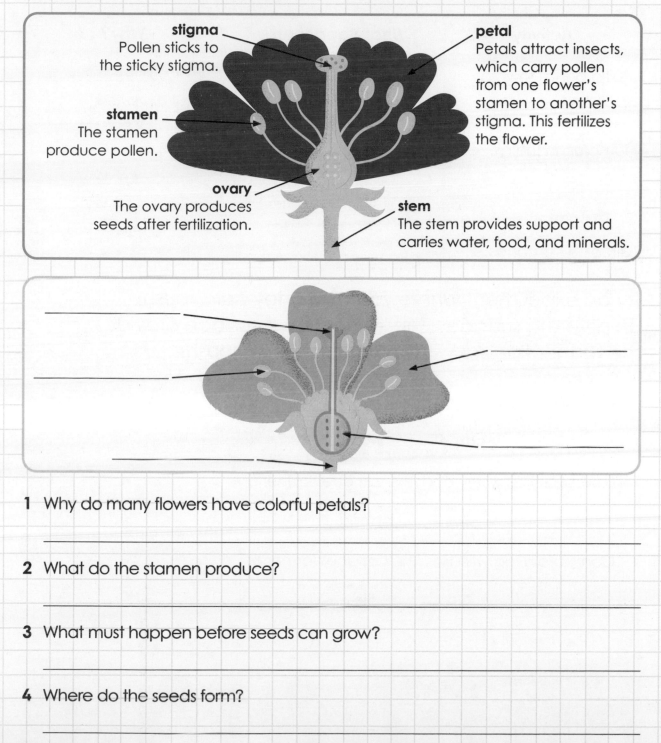

stigma
Pollen sticks to
the sticky stigma.

petal
Petals attract insects,
which carry pollen
from one flower's
stamen to another's
stigma. This fertilizes
the flower.

stamen
The stamen
produce pollen.

ovary
The ovary produces
seeds after fertilization.

stem
The stem provides support and
carries water, food, and minerals.

1 Why do many flowers have colorful petals?

_____

2 What do the stamen produce?

_____

3 What must happen before seeds can grow?

_____

4 Where do the seeds form?

_____

Gravity and Friction

Gravity is the force that pulls all objects toward the Earth. Friction is the force that acts when objects are in contact. It slows things down.

Try these activities, and complete the chart.

Activity	What Happened?	Why?
Roll a pencil toward the edge of a table.	The pencil rolled off and fell to the ground.	Gravity pulled the pencil downward.
Jump up in the air.		
Hold your arms in the air for 30 seconds.		

Try an experiment where you give a toy car a push on different surfaces. The less friction a surface provides, the farther the car will travel with just one push.

Compare carpet with wood. The car goes farther on

carpet   **wood**

Compare tiles with wood. The car goes farther on

tiles   **wood**

Compare a rug with tiles. The car goes farther on

rug   **tiles**

Force and Motion

An **object in motion** stays in motion, and an **object at rest** stays at rest, unless it's acted on by a force, such as gravity, friction, or a human action.

Write whether each object is in motion or at rest.

The ball is at rest.
_____   _____   _____

Sticker the correct words under each scene to show whether the force causes the object to speed up or slow down.

Gravity pulls on a ripe apple as it comes away from the branch.

A mountain bike's rough tires provide **friction** when it skids.

The girl hits the puck with the ice-hockey stick.

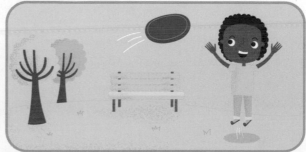

The boy catches the Frisbee as it passes.

Simple Machines

Simple machines help make work easier.

Use the word bank to fill in the blanks with the correct simple machine.

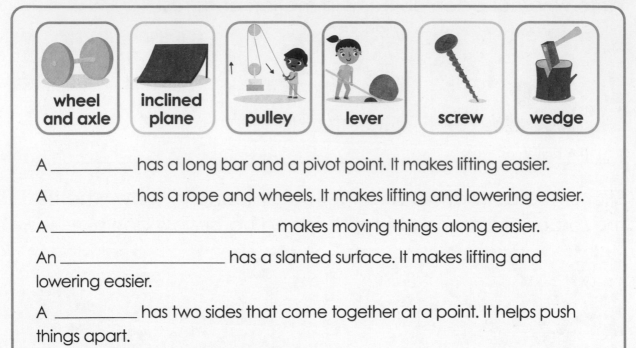

wheel and axle | inclined plane | pulley | lever | screw | wedge

A _____ has a long bar and a pivot point. It makes lifting easier.

A _____ has a rope and wheels. It makes lifting and lowering easier.

A _____ makes moving things along easier.

An _____ has a slanted surface. It makes lifting and lowering easier.

A _____ has two sides that come together at a point. It helps push things apart.

A _____ is a spiral-shaped inclined plane used to join things.

Circle the simple machine that would work best.

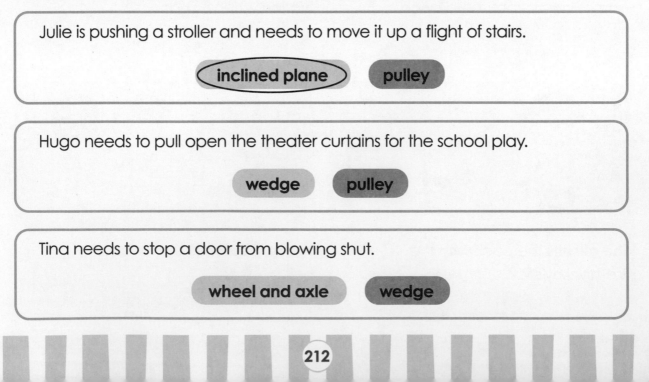

Julie is pushing a stroller and needs to move it up a flight of stairs.

(inclined plane)   pulley

Hugo needs to pull open the theater curtains for the school play.

wedge   pulley

Tina needs to stop a door from blowing shut.

wheel and axle   wedge

Complex Machines

When two or more simple machines work together, they create a complex machine.

Write either **simple** or **complex** under each machine.

_____ _____ _____ _____

For each complex machine, unscramble the letters to find the simple machines it contains.

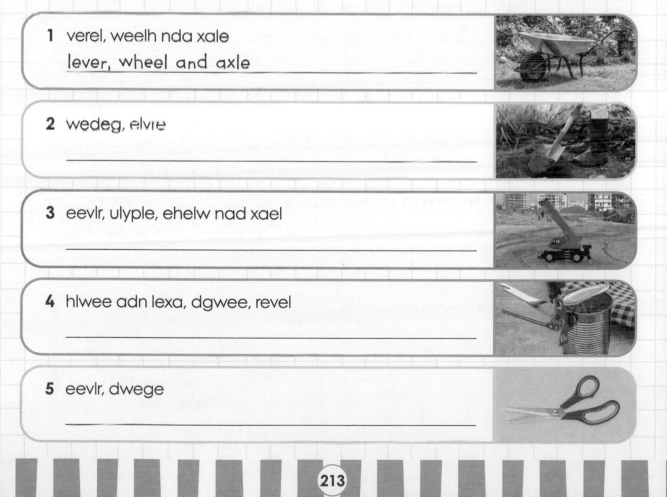

1 verel, weelh nda xale
lever, wheel and axle
_____

2 wedeg, elvre
_____

3 eevlr, ulyple, ehelw nad xael
_____

4 hlwee adn lexa, dgwee, revel
_____

5 eevlr, dwege
_____

Electricity

Electricity flows around a path called a **circuit**. A **closed circuit** has no breaks, which allows electricity to flow around it. An **open circuit** has a break that stops electricity flowing.

Label which diagram shows a closed circuit and which shows an open circuit. Then answer the questions.

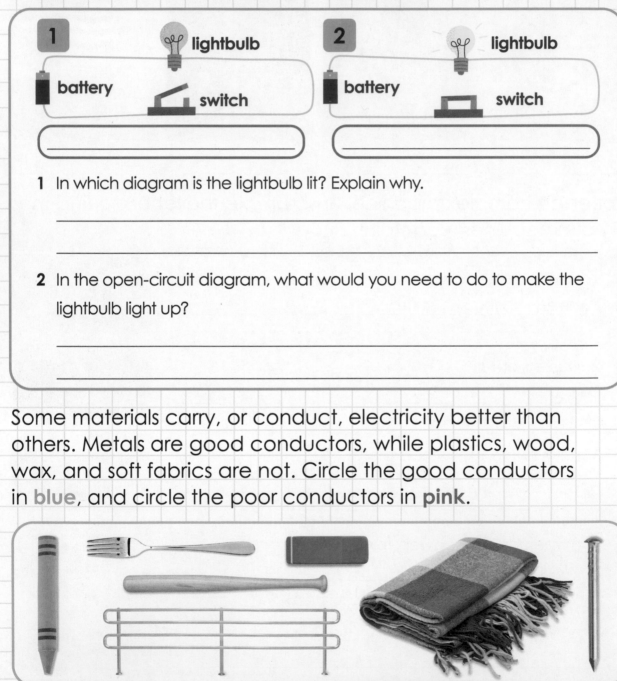

1 In which diagram is the lightbulb lit? Explain why.

_____

_____

2 In the open-circuit diagram, what would you need to do to make the lightbulb light up?

_____

_____

Some materials carry, or conduct, electricity better than others. Metals are good conductors, while plastics, wood, wax, and soft fabrics are not. Circle the good conductors in **blue**, and circle the poor conductors in **pink**.

Microscopes

Scientists use **microscopes** to see small things,
such as the cells that make up a living thing.

Look at these plant cells as seen through a microscope.
Draw what you see. Then write a short description.

Red Onion Cells	The Surface of a Leaf

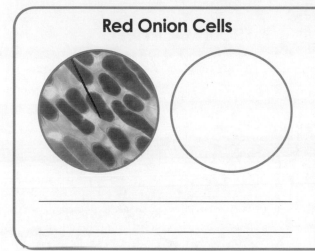

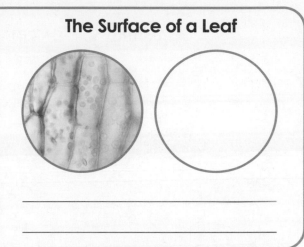

_____

_____

_____

_____

Electron microscopes can magnify images to a much greater
level than ordinary light microscopes. What do you think these
electron microscope images show?

Hint: We like to travel in long lines.

Hint: I'm sweet in a drink.

_____

_____

World Map

Earth has **seven continents**, or large land masses, and **five oceans**.

Unscramble the name of each continent.

ACARIF THORN ICAMERA POUREE ISAA

ASARITUAL CATRINACAT SHOUT MACIERA

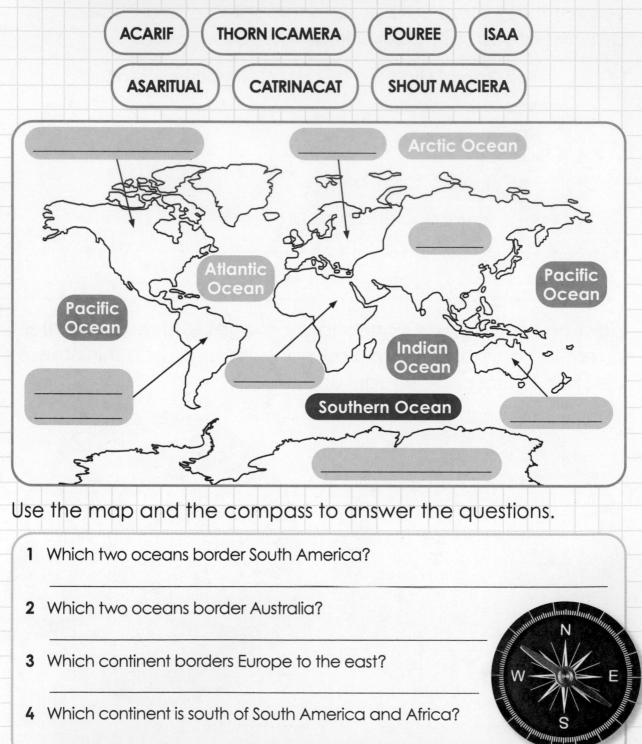

Arctic Ocean

Atlantic Ocean

Pacific Ocean

Pacific Ocean

Indian Ocean

Southern Ocean

Use the map and the compass to answer the questions.

1 Which two oceans border South America?

_____

2 Which two oceans border Australia?

_____

3 Which continent borders Europe to the east?

_____

4 Which continent is south of South America and Africa?

_____

Latitude and Longitude

> Lines of latitude circle the Earth, parallel to the Equator.
> Lines of longitude run from the north pole to the south pole.

Use the map to find the latitude and longitude of each letter.

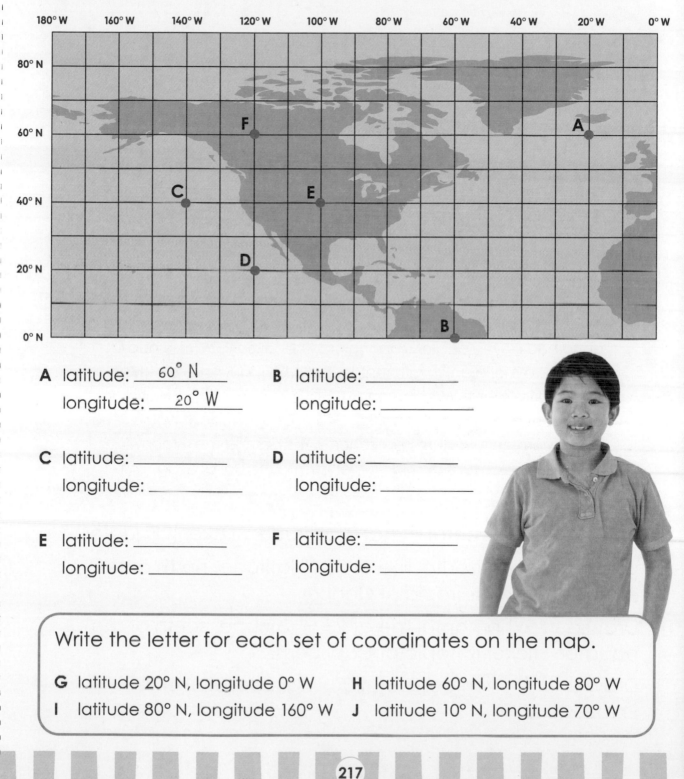

A latitude: _____60° N_____ **B** latitude: _____
longitude: _____20° W_____ longitude: _____

C latitude: _____ **D** latitude: _____
longitude: _____ longitude: _____

E latitude: _____ **F** latitude: _____
longitude: _____ longitude: _____

Write the letter for each set of coordinates on the map.

G latitude 20° N, longitude 0° W   **H** latitude 60° N, longitude 80° W

I latitude 80° N, longitude 160° W   **J** latitude 10° N, longitude 70° W

The Equator and
Prime Meridian

Read the text. Then draw the lines of latitude and longitude on the map on page 219.

Earth's **Equator** is an imaginary line encircling the planet. It lies halfway between the north pole and the south pole. Its latitude is 0°. Places along the Equator have twelve hours of daylight and twelve hours of night all year.

The **Tropic of Cancer** is a line that lies 23.5° north of the Equator, and the **Tropic of Capricorn** is a line that lies 23.5° south of the Equator. The parts of Earth that lie between these lines are called the tropics, and they have a hot climate.

Like the Equator, the **prime meridian** is an imaginary line, but unlike the Equator, it is not a natural midpoint. For many years, countries disagreed on the degrees of longitude because they assigned 0°, or the zero meridian, to different lines of longitude. Finally, in 1884, 25 countries met in Washington, D.C., at the International Meridian Conference to decide on a single line of 0° longitude. It would divide the eastern and western hemispheres. They chose the Greenwich Meridian, which runs through Greenwich in the United Kingdom.

Draw a **red** horizontal line at 0° latitude. Sticker it Equator.

Draw a **blue** horizontal line at 23.5° latitude, north of the equator. Sticker it Tropic of Cancer.

Draw a **blue** horizontal line at 23.5° latitude, south of the equator. Sticker it Tropic of Capricorn.

Draw a **green** vertical line at 0° longitude. Sticker it Prime Meridian.

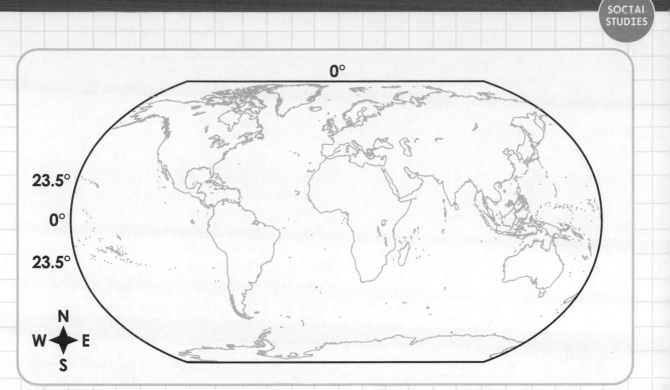

Use the text on page 218 to answer the questions.

1 All planets have an equator. What is an equator?

_____

_____

2 What type of climate do places between the Tropic of Capricorn and the Tropic of Cancer experience?

_____

3 True or false? At the Equator, daylight is longer in the summer and shorter in the winter.

_____

4 True or false? The prime meridian divides the world into the eastern and western hemispheres.

_____

5 In what year did the International Meridian Conference meet?

_____

6 Why is it important to have a single prime meridian?

_____

_____

Climate

Earth has five main climates: tropical, dry, temperate, continental, and polar.

Match each climate with its best description.

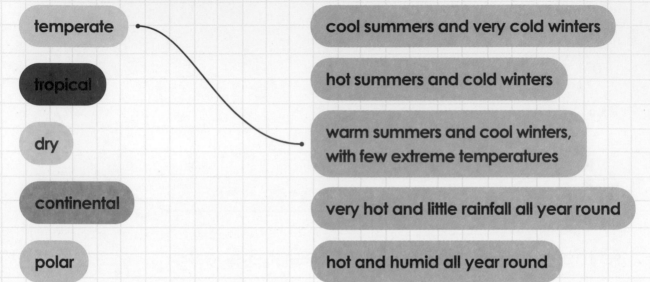

temperate

tropical

dry

continental

polar

cool summers and very cold winters

hot summers and cold winters

warm summers and cool winters, with few extreme temperatures

very hot and little rainfall all year round

hot and humid all year round

Use the key to shade the map. Some has been shaded already.

Key: 1 blue, 2 green, 3 orange, 4 red, 5 yellow

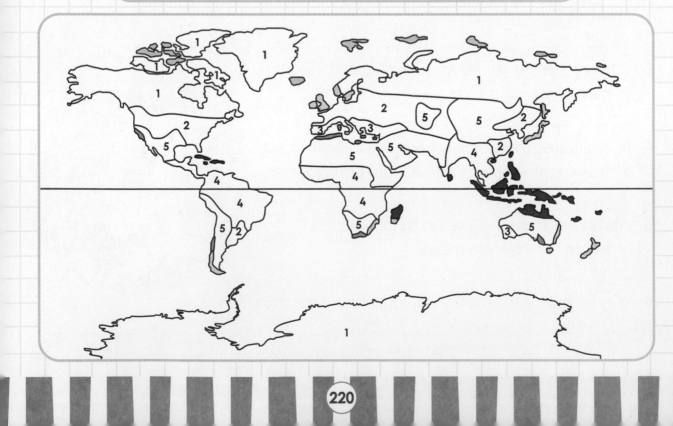

The 50 States

The United States is made up of **50 states**. Each state has its own capital city as well as an official bird, flower, motto, and flag.

Use books, encyclopedias, or the Internet to learn more about the state where you live, or a state you'd like to know more about.

State: _____

State capital: _____

State bird: _____

State flower: _____

State motto: _____

_____

Draw a picture of the state's flag.

Use the map to find the state. Circle it.

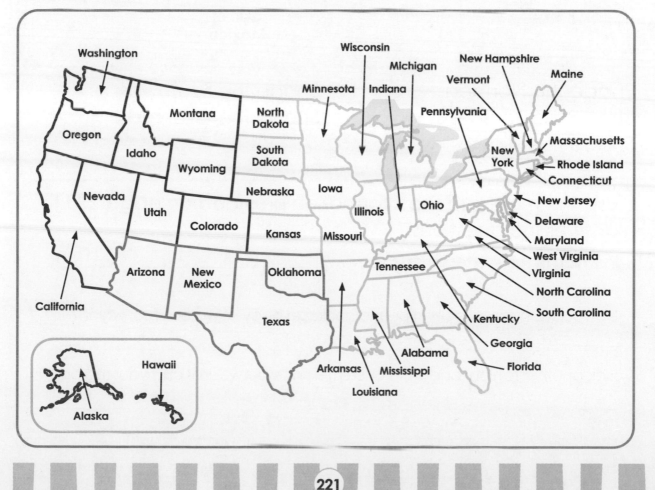

The Five US Regions

The **United States** is often divided into five regions: the **Northeast**, the **Southeast**, the **Midwest**, the **Southwest**, and the **West**.

The Northeast

The Midwest

The West

Pacific Ocean

The West

The Southwest

The Southeast

Atlantic Ocean

Gulf of Mexico

Shade the Northeast **blue**.
Shade the Southeast **yellow**.
Shade the Midwest **green**.

Shade the Southwest **pink**.
Shade the West **red**.

Use the map and the information provided on page 223 to answer the questions.

In which of the five regions do you live? _____

Do you live near an ocean or another large body of water? If so, which?

_____

Pick another region, and write one difference between it and your region.

_____

Read about the regions, and label the photos.

Statue of Liberty

The Northeast
- Climate: Often hot and humid in the summer and cold in the winter with some blizzards.
- Things to see: Niagara Falls, the Liberty Bell, the Statue of Liberty, the Adirondack Mountains, and the White House.

The Southeast
- Climate: Hot and humid in the summer with mild winters. Hurricanes are common between June and November.
- Things to see: Cape Canaveral, the Smoky Mountains, the Everglades, Fort Sumter, and Graceland.

The Midwest
- Climate: Hot and humid in the summer with cold and snowy winters. Blizzards and tornadoes are common.
- Things to see: Gateway Arch, Willis Tower, the Rock and Roll Hall of Fame, Mount Rushmore, and the Great Lakes.

The Southwest
- Climate: Semi-desert, usually with warm temperatures and low rainfall all year round.
- Things to see: The Alamo, the Rocky Mountains, the Grand Canyon, the Acoma Pueblo, and the Gulf of Mexico.

The West
- Climate: This region is diverse in its climate, and includes deserts, snowy mountains, and rainforests.
- Things to see: Yosemite National Park, the Golden Gate Bridge, the Hoover Dam, Death Valley, and Pearl Harbor.

The Declaration of
Independence

The Declaration of Independence, written by Thomas Jefferson in 1776, stated that the American colonies did not want to be ruled by the King of England. They wanted an independent government.

Read these lines from the Declaration of Independence. Use a dictionary to look up the words in **bold** and write their meanings. Then answer the questions.

We hold these truths to be **self-evident**, that all men are created equal, that they are **endowed** by their Creator with certain **unalienable** Rights, that among these are Life, Liberty and the **pursuit** of Happiness.

Word	Meaning
self-evident	
endowed	
unalienable	
pursuit	

1 Who wrote the Declaration of Independence?

_____

2 Why was the Declaration of Independence written?

_____
_____
_____
_____

IN CONGRESS. JULY 4. 1776.

The unanimous Declaration of the thirteen united States of America

The Constitution

Read the text, and then answer the questions.

After the American colonies won their independence from England, they created a new government called a republic. The US Constitution sets out the basic laws of the government. It was written by James Madison and signed on September 17, 1787. In addition to the Constitution, the Bill of Rights guarantees certain rights for all American citizens, including freedom of speech and the right to a fair trial.

1 What type of government does the United States of America have?

monarchy   republic   confederation

2 Which document guarantees certain rights for American citizens?

Bill of Rights   Declaration of Independence   Articles of Confederation

3 In what year was the Constitution signed?

1776   1787   1789

Find the words in the word search.

Madison
Constitution
Bill of Rights
Republic
Government

R	M	A	D	X	O	A	N	M	L	M	I	N	T	U
E	V	C	I	A	V	W	R	A	Q	M	E	T	Y	W
P	R	U	L	G	M	I	B	D	E	O	N	O	C	F
U	G	I	C	O	N	S	T	I	T	U	T	I	O	N
B	L	O	H	V	C	T	R	S	L	P	X	Y	N	J
L	U	G	V	R	E	E	O	O	S	D	A	I	S	O
I	O	S	C	E	B	A	T	N	B	E	P	B	T	L
C	S	A	U	D	R	T	L	P	U	E	V	H	G	T
E	R	L	M	B	L	N	Y	I	C	F	K	N	W	A
O	W	K	A	G	O	V	M	C	I	S	Q	U	N	Z
A	F	C	D	Z	E	J	R	E	P	U	N	I	O	A
H	J	A	I	I	N	E	U	A	N	E	O	R	I	U
B	I	L	L	O	F	R	I	G	H	T	S	B	U	E

Branches of Government

Read the text, and then answer the questions.

> The United States has three parts, or branches, of government. The three branches work together to govern the country.
>
> The **Legislative Branch** makes the laws. It is made up of the US Senate and the US House of Representatives, which together form Congress.
>
> The President of the United States is the head of the **Executive Branch**, which enforces national, or federal, laws.
>
> The **Judicial Branch** interprets the laws. The Supreme Court decides whether laws agree with the US Constitution. The Supreme Court is made up of nine members, or justices. Once chosen by the president and approved by the US Senate, a justice can serve for life.

1 What are the three branches of government?

_____

_____

2 Who is the head of the Executive Branch?

_____

3 The Legislative Branch is made up of _____

_____

4 What does the Judicial Branch do?

_____

_____

Label the three branches of government.

_____

_____   _____

Local Government

Local governments are responsible for making decisions that affect particular cities, towns, or regions.

Write a letter to your mayor or a local representative to let them know about an issue in your community. Be sure to include why this issue is important and provide a suggestion for solving it.

Choose from one of the issues in the box or pick one of your own.

the environment   local parks   road safety   community center

Write your address here. ———————

Write the date here. ———————

Write the name of the person here. ———

Dear _____

_____

_____

_____

_____

_____

Sign your name here.

Yours truly, _____

Citizenship

You can become an **American citizen** by being born in the United States of America, by having an American parent, or by taking a citizenship test.

Read the text, and then complete the chart.

American citizens have certain rights, but non-citizens have rights, too. Citizens have the right to vote. You need to be an American citizen to run for a public office such as state governor and to hold most government jobs. Only people born in the United States can run for president. You don't need to be a citizen to have a driver's license, buy a house, or have a job.

American Citizens' Rights	Non-American Citizens' Rights

You do not need to be born in the United States to run for president. **true / false**

You need to be a citizen to buy a house in the United States. **true / false**

The Haudenosaunee

Read the text, and then answer the questions.

The **Haudenosaunee** (or the Iroquois) is a confederacy of six nations in the eastern Great Lakes region and beyond. The nations are the Mohawk, Oneida, Onondaga, Cayuga, Seneca, and Tuscarora. They were united by a great leader called The Peacemaker. In the past, large, extended families related on the mother's side lived together in longhouses. Like many agricultural tribes in North America, they grew three main crops—corn, beans, and squash—also known as the three sisters.

1 What are the six nations of the Haudenosaunee?

_____

_____

2 Where do the Haudenosaunee mainly live?

_____

3 How were the people who lived in each longhouse related?

_____

4 What are the three sisters?

_____

The Cherokee

Read the text, and then answer the questions.

The **Cherokee** homelands are in present-day South Carolina, North Carolina, Georgia, and Tennessee. When they lived there, they often lived in wattle-and-daub houses, which were made of thin branches and mud. They grew corn, beans, and squash and hunted and fished. In the 1830s, the US army forced the Cherokee people to move to Oklahoma, over 1,000 miles away. More than 4,000 people died on the march west, known as the Cherokee Trail of Tears.

The Cherokee Trail of Tears

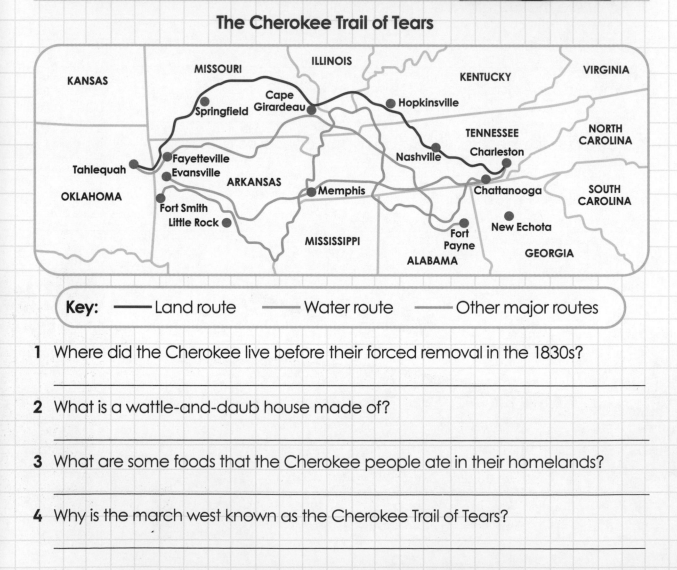

Key: —— Land route   —— Water route   —— Other major routes

1 Where did the Cherokee live before their forced removal in the 1830s?

_____

2 What is a wattle-and-daub house made of?

_____

3 What are some foods that the Cherokee people ate in their homelands?

_____

4 Why is the march west known as the Cherokee Trail of Tears?

_____
_____

The Great Sioux Nation

Read the text, and then answer the questions.

> The **Great Sioux Nation** is made up of the Dakota, the Lakota, and the Nakota speaking peoples. Many years before Europeans arrived, the Sioux peoples lived in present-day North Dakota, South Dakota, Wisconsin, and Minnesota. They were nomadic, meaning they moved to follow their main food source, the bison, or buffalo. They also used the bison to make their clothing, tools, and shelter. Sitting Bull and Crazy Horse were two of many Lakota Sioux chiefs who fought against the US government's takeover of their lands.

1 Name the three main tribes of the Great Sioux Nation.

_____

_____

2 What does nomadic mean?

_____

_____

Crazy Horse

3 Other than for food, why did the Sioux people hunt bison?

_____

_____

4 Who were Sitting Bull and Crazy Horse?

_____

_____

Sitting Bull

History Timeline

Historians work with **dates** to figure out the order in which **past events** happened.

Use the timeline to answer the questions.

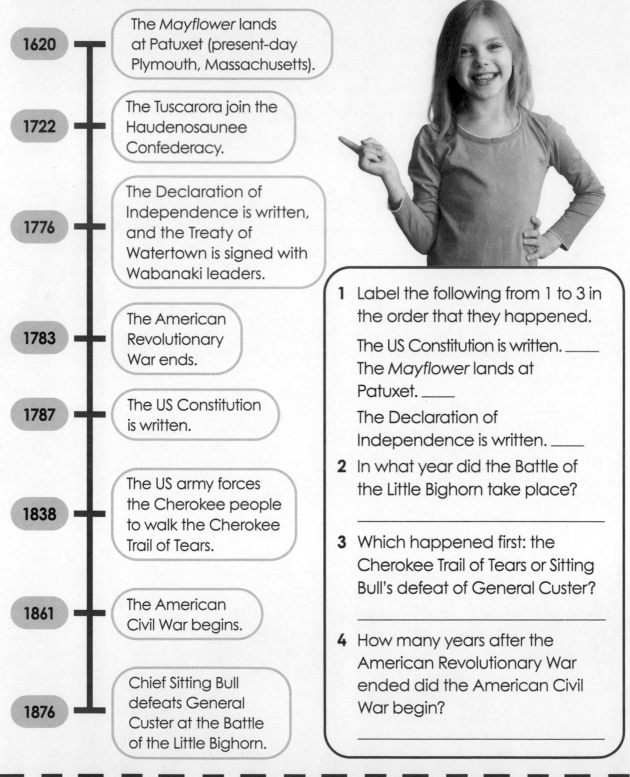

1620 — The *Mayflower* lands at Patuxet (present-day Plymouth, Massachusetts).

1722 — The Tuscarora join the Haudenosaunee Confederacy.

1776 — The Declaration of Independence is written, and the Treaty of Watertown is signed with Wabanaki leaders.

1783 — The American Revolutionary War ends.

1787 — The US Constitution is written.

1838 — The US army forces the Cherokee people to walk the Cherokee Trail of Tears.

1861 — The American Civil War begins.

1876 — Chief Sitting Bull defeats General Custer at the Battle of the Little Bighorn.

1 Label the following from 1 to 3 in the order that they happened.

The US Constitution is written. _____

The *Mayflower* lands at Patuxet. _____

The Declaration of Independence is written. _____

2 In what year did the Battle of the Little Bighorn take place?

_____

3 Which happened first: the Cherokee Trail of Tears or Sitting Bull's defeat of General Custer?

_____

4 How many years after the American Revolutionary War ended did the American Civil War begin?

_____

Famous Americans

Read the text. Then complete the Venn diagram to show the similarities and differences between the two historical figures.

Abigail Adams

Abigail Adams was the second first lady of the United States (1797 until 1801). She was married to President John Adams. Abigail and John Adams wrote long letters to one another. She urged him to remember the importance of women's rights when creating the new US government. She also believed every person had the right to a good education.

Eleanor Roosevelt

Eleanor Roosevelt was the thirty-second first lady of the United States (from 1933 until 1945). She was married to President Franklin Delano Roosevelt. Eleanor and Franklin worked closely together to help unemployed people and struggling businesses during the Great Depression in the 1930s. After her husband died, she continued to campaign for civil rights, women's rights, and workers' rights.

Abigail Adams   **Eleanor Roosevelt**

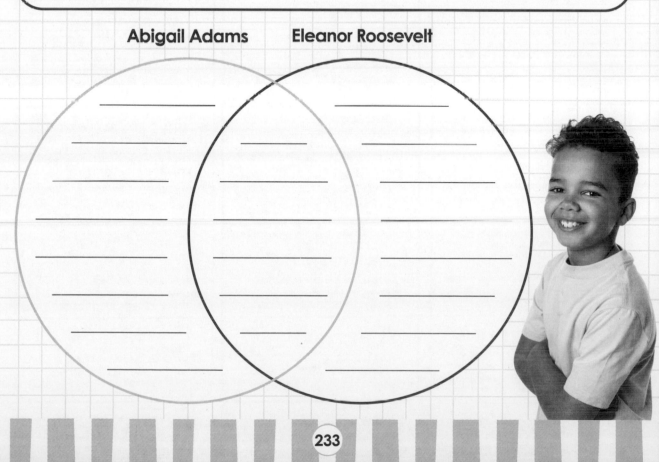

Answers

Reading

P5 Harmful chemicals called pesticides are killing bees. ✓; Bees transport pollen between flowers. ✓; Honeybees live in hives made up of thousands of insects. **X**; A bee lying on the ground may need food. ✓; Honeybees tell one another where to find food by doing a waggle dance. **X**

p6 Red box = beginning; green box = ending; blue box = climax; beginning, climax, ending

p7 **Blue box:** Ye Xian is the main character. The story is set long ago in a cave village. The main problem is that Ye Xian is bullied by her stepfamily. They stop her going to the New Year Festival.

Yellow box: The most exciting moment is when Ye Xian sees her stepfamily at the festival and is scared they will recognize her. Ye Xian faces her problem by running away and leaving behind her golden slipper.

Red box: The problem is resolved when a king looks for the owner of the slipper. When Ye Xian tries on the shoe, it fits perfectly, and she lives happily ever after with the king.

P8

Lola		Luke	
feelings	traits	feelings	traits
angry	generous	excited	friendly
grumpy	friendly	bored	forgetful
happy	determined	worried	
		happy	

P9 1 London, 2 midnight, 3 more than 100 years ago, 4 wind, thunder, rain, shivered, gust

P10 **Blue/literal** = Gabriel put on his headphones and danced around his bedroom.
Jacob ripped the packet and spilled the beans all over the floor.
Grace ate a piece of cake at her surprise birthday party.

Orange/figurative = Emily couldn't keep her secret, so she spilled the beans to Madison. **I**
The car's engine grumbled as Mr. Smith turned the key in the ignition. **P**
Isabelle was so hungry she could have eaten an elephant. **H**
Logan finished his test quickly because it was a piece of cake. **I**
The icy air was filled with dancing snowflakes. **P**
Cameron's smile was a mile wide. **H**

P11 Wording may vary but they must include *like* or *as*. The baby behaved like an angel all day.
Mrs. Jenkins was as angry as a volcano, ready to explode.

P12 Row 1 = first image, row 2 = second image, row 3 = first image, row 4 = third image

P13 1 He wanted to embarrass the stork because he thought she looked odd. **2** She wanted to teach the fox a lesson by tricking him just as he had tricked her. **3** Treat others as you would like to be treated.

P14 1 Loki had to choose between fetching Idun or losing his life. **2** The gods needed Idun because without her golden apples they were starting to age. **3** It explains how the Norse gods stayed young.

P15 1 Examples could include: Fire was owned by Bear. Bear carried Fire. "Feed me! Feed me!" he cried. "Please bring me sticks and twigs to eat," said Fire. They were happy together. Fire was angry and chased her away.
2 Answer could relate to enjoying the continuation of old traditions.

P16 1 Who has seen the wind? **2** The repetition emphasizes the mystery of the wind. **3** The leaves hang trembling. The trees bow down their heads.
4 quatrain (4 lines), **5** mysterious, powerful

P17 1 set 1: beard, feared, beard, set 2: Hen, Wren

P18 Come and try the tastiest ice cream in town! **O**
We open on Saturday at 11:00 a.m. **F**
We have more than 50 flavors on sale. **F**
Kids will love building their own sundaes. **O**
Once you try our ice cream, you'll never buy another brand again. **O**
One scoop costs $1.99. **F**, Two scoops cost $2.99. **F**
Get a free topping with your first purchase. **F**

P19 1 Yes, **2** reason 1: Movies stop people being creative; reason 2: Books are more detailed than movies; reason 3: Reading is a better way to relax before bed.

P20 Order of instructions: 1, 5, 3, 4, 6, 7, 2

P21 Missing dates: 1944, 1963; Missing facts: King organizes the Montgomery Bus Boycott. King wins the Nobel Peace Prize.

P22 **Text 1:** written by students, persuasive writing, written for the principal; **Overlap:** mentions uniforms being neat, is about school uniforms; **Text 2:** written by a journalist, written for the public, informative writing

P23 1 Text 1: letter; Text 2: newspaper article, **2** The author's purpose was to persuade the principal to reverse the decision to make students wear uniforms. **3** The author's purpose was to inform people about the change in uniform policy. **4** Text 2 presents both sides, and Text 1 is more one-sided.

Writing

P24 *Tyrannosaurus rex was one of the fiercest dinosaurs on Earth.* It hunted other animals, which means it was a predator. *T. rex* also had a huge body that could grow up to 40 feet long. That's about as long as a school bus! Each one of *T. rex's* sharp teeth was the size of a banana. This is why *T. rex* was called "king of the tyrant lizards."
✓ My favorite sport is baseball.

P26 why, who, when, how.

P27 fable, humor, science fiction, mystery, fantasy, adventure

P31
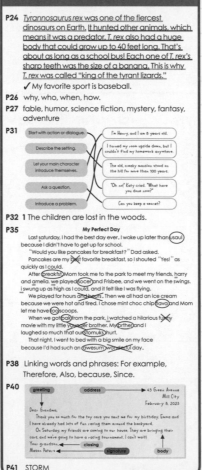

Start with action or dialogue.	I'm Henry, and I am 8 years old.
Describe the setting.	I turned my room upside down, but I couldn't find my homework anywhere.
Let your main character introduce themselves.	The old, creaky mansion stood on the hill for more than 100 years.
Ask a question.	"Oh no!" Katy cried. "What have you done now?"
Introduce a problem.	Can you keep a secret?

P32 1 The children are lost in the woods.

P35

My Perfect Day

Last saturday, I had the best day ever. I woke up later than (usual) because I didn't have to get up for school.
"Would you like pancakes for breakfast?" Dad asked.
Pancakes are my best favorite breakfast, so I shouted "Yes!" as quickly as I could.
After (breakfast) Mom took me to the park to meet my friends. harry and amelia. we played (soccer) and Frisbee, and we went on the swings. i swung up as high as I could, and it felt like I was flying.
We played for hours and hours. Then we all had an ice cream because we were hot and tired. I chose mint choc chip (flava) and Mom let me have (too) scoops.
When we got (bak) from the park, i watched a hilarious (funny) movie with my little younger brother. My (brother) and I laughed so much that our (stomuks) hurt.
That night, I went to bed with a big smile on my face because I'd had such an (awesum) (wonderful) day.

P38 Linking words and phrases: For example, Therefore, Also, because, Since.

P40

greeting — Dear Grandma,
address — 43 Green Avenue, Mill City
February 8, 2023
Thank you so much for the toy cars you sent me for my birthday, Emma and I have already had lots of fun racing them around the backyard.
On Saturday, my friends are coming to our house. They are bringing their cars, and we're going to have a racing tournament. I can't wait!
closing — Your grandson,
signature — Mason Peters
body

P41 STORM

Grammar and Punctuation

P42 Answers will vary. These nouns should be changed for other nouns. **2** France, skateboard, **3** waves, beach, **4** daisies, Mom, **5** phone, table, **6** children, candy, **7** glitter, picture, **8** spaghetti, soda.

P43 **Proper nouns:** Alex Davis, *The Three Little Pigs*, Fido, New Year's Day, Scholastic, Colorado, Abby Green, Golden Bay, Ben's Bakery, Italy, Albany, Asia, Mount Everest, July.
Improper nouns: bakery, weekend, oak tree, woman, boy, mountain, poodles, backyard, beach, summer, juice, rabbit, birthday, nonfiction books.

P44 1 two dishes, two buses, two matches, two kisses, two boxes, two glasses, two peaches, **2** two cities, two ponies, two skies, **3** two women, two loaves, two teeth, two children, two geese, two oases, two feet, two leaves, two oxen.

P45 The man's foot, the girl's laugh, the tree's roots, the house's roof, Lucy's bike
The exact wording may vary. **2** I'm looking for the dog's leash. **3** I'm staying at my grandmother's house. **4** The ship's deck was battered by the waves. **5** The book's title is *Pirate Adventure*. **6** We laughed at all Mateo's jokes.

P46 the babies' toys, the dogs' dinners, the rabbits' hutch, the Wilsons' house, the bananas' skins, the fish's tails, the geese's feathers, the people's bags, the children's lunch, the fishermen's boats, **2** I met Emilia in the dentists' waiting room. **3** Where is the women's changing room? **4** The fungi's caps are red with white spots.

P47 2 You, **3** They, **4** It, **5** we, **6** She
2 We are playing a computer game.
3 They are away on vacation. **4** It is brand new.
5 She wants to buy the next book in the series.

P48 2 us, **3** her, **4** it, **5** me, **6** you **2** Dad hid it in his closet. **3** I talked to them. **4** We gave him a surprise party. **5** The rain soaked us.

P49 2 My, **3** our, **4** his, his, **5** her, my, **6** your, our
2 I found her missing false teeth. **3** That's their blue car. **4** I saw its mast swaying in the wind.
5 I wish I had her bravery.

P50 2 mine, **3** hers, **4** yours, **5** Theirs
2 This is my seat, and that's yours. **3** I think this car might be theirs. **4** Your dog is a poodle, and ours is a terrier. **5** Do you think this office is hers?

P51 2 Dad jumped when I gave him a fright.
3 Livvy ate pizza while she watched TV.
4 The Smiths are here. I invited them for dinner.
5 The truck kept going until it reached the depot.
2 their **3** she **4** her **5** they

P52 2 Jaden wore his (striped) T-shirt with his (orange) shorts.
3 Why is that (huge) hippo making that (loud) noise?
4 I baked (round) cookies and (rectangular) brownies.
5 The chips are (salty) and the fish is (fresh).
6 The frog felt (slimy) and the toad felt (bumpy).
7 Today, the weather is (cold) and (windy).
8 I've got (five) dollars and (a few) coins.
9 Look at that (funny) (fluffy) rabbit!

P53 2 Harper (is) (visiting) her best friend.
3 I (was) (working) hard.
4 Noah (has) (finished) his homework.
5 You (must) (help) Jamie.
6 She (should) (ask) Connor.
7 I (can) (ride) a skateboard.
8 We (were) (thinking) about you.

P54 **How:** gently, carefully, loudly, slowly, wildly, safely, enormously, shyly

when: frequently, tomorrow, always, now, soon, sometimes, then, yesterday
Where: far, up, everywhere, down, anywhere, inside, nowhere

P55 1 future, 2 past, 3 future, 4 present, 5 past, 6 present
1 walked, 2 will visit, 3 plays, 4 watched, 5 rushes, 6 will ride

P56 2 Isaac dances, 3 Hailey writes. 4 It sits on the shelf. 5 This cat sleeps all day. 6 My mother jumps on the trampoline. 7 Henry Jones is dreaming about soccer.
1 Looks good. X, 2 She thinks. ✓, 3 The wild, ragged beast. X, 4 Running very fast. X, 5 The apple slowly rots ✓, 6 Peter, Lizzie, and Luke. X

P57 1 compound, 2 simple, 3 compound, 4 simple, 5 compound, 6 simple,
1 compound, 2 complex, 3 compound, 4 complex, 5 complex, 6 compound

P58

Adjective	Comparative	Superlative
long	longer	longest
slow	slower	slowest
large	larger	largest
fine	finer	finest
happy	happier	happiest
busy	busier	busiest
sad	sadder	saddest
hot	hotter	hottest
good	better	best
bad	worse	worst
popular	more popular	most popular
interesting	more interesting	most interesting

When a word ends in **-e**, just add -r or -st. When an adjective ends in -y, change the y to an **I**, before adding -er or -est. For consonant-vowel-consonant (CVC) words, double the last **letter**, before adding -er or -est. For words of three or more syllables, use *more* to make the comparative and use **most** to make the superlative.

P59 1 or, 2 but, 3 and, 4 so, 5 yet, 6 nor
1 After, 2 because, 3 until, 4 although, 5 while, 6 before

P60 2 When you're ready, you can join the game.
3 Before I met you, I didn't know any famous people.
4 After we eat, we should watch a movie.
5 While you're away, I will call you every day.
2 Without thinking, he rushed to the baby's rescue.
3 Last week, my brother passed his driving test.
4 In 2012, my parents met at a party.
5 If there's room, you can come with us.

P61 2 Mom said, "Let's go to the lake tomorrow."
3 "I'd love to work with computers," Lily said.
4 Mrs. Evans announced, "We are going to put on a play."
5 "I'd like to be a vet," said Daniel.
Exact wording may vary.
2 Arianna said, "I feel too tired to keep going."
3 Josiah shouted, "Maddie, watch out for the cars!"

Vocab and Spelling

p62 2 mistrust, 3 uncomfortable, 4 dishonest, 5 insecure, 6 misspell, 7 unknown, 8 disagree, 9 misbehave, 10 improper, 11 impossible, 12 inactive

P63 2 underwater, 3 recycle, 4 preplan, 5 nonsense, 6 decode, 7 reappear, 8 overdone, 9 underline, 10 premade, 11 defrost, 12 overheard

P64 2 cheered, 3 visited, 4 cried.

P65 violinist, magician, comedian, juggler, pianist, dancer, rapper, actor, director

P66

Word	Root Word	Root Word Definition
activity	active	busy or energetic
impolite	polite	having good manners
powerful	power	control or authority
youngster	young	at an early stage of life
incorrect	correct	right or accurate
lovely	love	strong affection
addition	add	to join two or more numbers

P67 milkshake, earthworm, skateboard, teardrop, afternoon, ponytail, fireplace, aircraft, somewhere.
limestone, notebook, peanut, downhill, handshake.

P68 loud crowd, small fall, mad dad, quick pick
Exact synonyms used may vary. 2 Mateo shouted and screamed when he banged his leg. Mateo yelled when he banged his leg. 3 Owen chuckled and giggled while reading his book. Owen laughed while reading his book. 4 Charlotte bought gorgeous dresses and pretty shoes. Charlotte bought beautiful dresses and shoes. 5 Avery was sleepy and drowsy after a long day at the park. Avery was tired after a long day at the park.

P69 Blue flags: furious/angry; almost/nearly; smart/clever.
Orange flags: day/night; early/late; whisper/shout; young/old; start/finish; seldom/often.
Exact antonyms may vary. 2 Xander's cup was full. 3 Anna couldn't stop crying at the movie. 4 Ezra always remembers his friends' birthdays. 5 Savannah is the tallest girl in the class.

P70 read, reed; flour, flower; knight, night; pair, pear; write, right.
2 The plane flew over the dusty plain. 3 The herd of antelope heard the lion coming. 4 Sam rode his horse down the long road. 5 The grizzly bear slept under a tree that was bare of leaves.

P71 bark, park, rock, ruler
Exact wording of definitions may vary. Ethan turned right because he was sure it was the right way. 1 a direction that is the opposite of left, 2 true or correct
Did the store close to our house close? 1 near, 2 to shut down.
Grandma rose from her chair to water her rose. 1 stood up, 2 a type of flower.
Elijah pressed his palm against the rough trunk of the palm tree. 1 the inner surface of the hand. 2 a tropical tree

P72 little, bubble, cherry, ribbon, correct, bottle, kitten, different, summer, funny, puddle, matter, manner, or madder, lesson, embarrass

Word	Add -ed.	Add -ing.
stop	stopped	stopping
grin	grinned	grinning
box	boxed	boxing
pop	popped	popping
mix	mixed	mixing
relax	relaxed	relaxing
blur	blurred	blurring

P73 sh: short, shock, ship, rush; ch: choice, church, child, such; th: math, thumb, thank, both; wh: whale, whirl, why, whisk; ph: phone, graph, phonics; ng: string, wing, fang, song.
Exact wording of definitions may vary. chew: to tear or grind with your teeth; what: a question word asking for information about someone or something; tooth: a hard white object in the mouth, used for biting and chewing; young: at an early stage of life; health: without sickness or pain.

P75 2 Isla gnawed on the knob of butter. 3 The knight guarded the guilty ghost. 4 Who wrote the rhyming answer? 5 A lamb sang hymns for an hour. 6 I sailed my yacht to a gnome's island.

P76 yellow/ar words: car, market, hard, chart, farm; blue/er words: her, serve, germ, person; green/or words: sport, morning, pork, fork, storm; red /ir words: first, girl, twirl, circle; purple/ur words: curl, turn, hurt, turtle, nurse.

P77 2 e / el / phant — elephant
3 Sat / day / ur — Saturday
4 tween / be — between
5 por / im / tant — important
6 li / cop / he / ter — helicopter
7 wich / sand — sandwich
8 mul / ca / ti / tion / pli — multiplication
9 cit / ex / ing — exciting
10 cat / er / lar / pil — caterpillar
11 ing / pen / hap — happening
12 tions / grat / u / la / con — congratulations

P78 worried, cold, hate, angry, helped
1 good 2 great 3 perfect
1 irritated 2 angry 3 furious
1 jogged 2 ran 3 sprinted
1 worried 2 scared 3 terrified

P79 1 a river or stream that flows into or out of a larger river, 2 a pleasant smell, 3 very cold, 4 unstable or in a risky position, 5 heard or able to be heard, 6 a large number that is more than enough, believable, 7 complicated and confusing, to explain or make easier to understand

Research

P82 Fiction: Alice's Adventures in Wonderland, Gulliver's Travels, Frankenstein; Nonfiction: Fearsome Dinosaur Facts, Fun Crossword Puzzles, Terrific Tiger Trivia

P83 1 Visit a Volcano, 2 page 14, 3 Mount Vesuvius, Mauna Loa, Krakatoa, 4 Chapter 4: What Happens When a Volcano Erupts?

P84 1 15–16, 30, 2 14, 29, 3 information about the Cretaceous Period, 4 Brachiosaurus and Claosaurus

P86 Antarctica = the continent where penguins live, emperor = the largest type of penguin, endangered = a species that is in danger of going extinct, herring = a type of fish

p87 1 parent, 2 click, 3 adult, 4 password, 5 personal, 6 buy
Good passwords: 34sgide$, Pb_j0515l, Rf16%*zh; bad passwords: 16June2017, fossilsarecool, KateBrown

p88 Best websites/green: uspresidents.gov, thewashingtonproject.org; websites that might be reliable/yellow: georgewashington.com, presidentwashington.net; websites you shouldn't use/red: goergewashignton.com, ilovegeorgewashington.net
Source 1: As a toddler, Helen Keller became sick and lost her eyesight and hearing. A young teacher called Anne Sullivan helped Helen learn to read and write. The two remained friends for life.
Source 2: Helen Keller could not speak or hear. Anne Sullivan, who had been blind but regained her eyesight through surgery, is known as the "miracle worker" because she taught Helen to read and write. Helen became an author.

P89 ad, informational
What do penguins eat?

What is the largest ocean in the world?
What different types of seals are there?
To what age do dolphins usually live?

P90 top row: point of view, point of view, bottom row: news, point of view, news

The Blizzard of 1996 hit on January 6 and lasted for two days. It snowed thirty inches in Philadelphia, and many roads closed. The temperature dropped below 0° Fahrenheit. I was eight years old, and it was the coldest winter I can remember. We had three days off school because of the snow, and I built a snowman with my friends. It was a magical time!

Number Practice

P98 4,167, 2,605

	thousands	hundreds	tens	ones
5,823	5	8	2	3
8,293	8	2	9	3
2,737	2	7	3	7
5,026	5	0	2	6
8,520	8	5	2	0
9,302	9	3	0	2
900		9	0	0

P99 90, 8,000, 7, 400
8,694, 2,859, 6,266, 3,902, 2,460, 4,052
9,735, 5,408, 7,613, 9,990

P100 two-thousand, six-hundred, ninety-four; four-thousand, six-hundred, twenty-eight; six-thousand, eight-hundred, two; three-thousand, fifty-five; seven-thousand, five-hundred, twenty; two-thousand, three
5,000 + 700 + 90 + 1; 2,000 + 600 + 40 + 7; 8,000 + 200 + 6; 7,000 + 700 + 30; 4,000 + 10 + 8; 6,000 + 2; 9,000 + 900 + 90 + 9; 1,000 + 200 + 30 + 4; 6,000 + 300

p101 8,235 > 836; 2,380 > 2,379; 7,023 < 7,203; 3,000 > 2,999; 5,283 < 5,292; 10,000 > 9,999; 2,350 > 2,305; 2,500 > 2,055; 7,001 < 7,010
5,349 5,999 6,340 6,346 6,400
9,000 9,028 9,208 9,999 10,000
999 1,000 1,010 1,100 1,110
5,005 5,505 5,555 5,564 5,999
1,923 2,034 4,628 6,203 7,234
28 237 1,101 6,000 10,000

P102 No, Amy has $789, which is less than the $800 she needs for the bike.
Yes, 4,011 is less than 5,010, so all the drivers will find a space.
She buys 3,520 pieces of fruit.
5,060
5,007
The bank teller will give Mark ten $100 bills because 10 x 100 = 1,000

P103 (10) **12** 20 30 **38** (40) 10 **19** (20)
(90) **92** 100 40 **45** (50) (70) **74** 80
(80) **83** 90 (20) **22** 30 (50) **54** 60
90 **99** (100)
70, 20, 90, 90, 10
30, 90, 30, 80, 80
Jack earned $30.

P104 700 **782** (800) (100) **115** 200
(300) **347** 400 900 **994** (1,000)
400 **483** (500) (500) **545** 600
(800) **825** 900 100 **160** (200)
(200) **229** 300 (400) **449** 500
400 100 300 900 300
900 600 700 500 500
Ella put $600 on the price tag.

P105 74 + 12 = (70 + 10) + (4 + 2) = **80** + **6** = **86**
62 + 33 = (**60** + **30**) + (**2** + **3**) = **90** + **5** = **95**
54 + 85 = (**50** + **80**) + (**4** + **5**) = **130** + **9** = **139**
26 + 92 = (**20** + **90**) + (**6** + **2**) = **110** + **8** = **118**
73 + 55 = (**70** + **50**) + (**3** + **5**) = **120** + **8** = **128**
56 + 64 = (**50** + **60**) + (**6** + **4**) = **110** + **10** = **120**
37 + 25 = (**30** + **20**) + (**7** + **5**) = **50** + **12** = **62**
46 + 27 = (**40** + **20**) + (**6** + **7**) = **60** + **13** = **73**

P106 341 + 443 = (300 + 400) + (40 + 40) + (1 + 3) = **700** + **80** + **4** = **784**
724 + 135 = (700 + 100) + (**20** + **30**) + (**4** + **5**) = **800** + **50** + **9** = **859**
356 + 417 = (300 + 400) + (**50** + **10**) + (**6** + **7**) = **700** + **60** + **13** = **773**
624 + 731 = (600 + 700) + (**20** + **30**) + (**4** + **1**) = **1,300** + **50** + **5** = **1,355**
855 + 423 = (800 + 400) + (**50** + **20**) + (**5** + **3**) = **1,200** + **70** + **8** = **1,278**
465 + 328 = (400 + 300) + (**60** + **20**) + (**5** + **8**) = **700** + **80** + **13** = **793**
282 + 543 = (200 + 500) + (**80** + **40**) + (**2** + **3**) = **700** + **120** + **5** = **825**
723 + 194 = (700 + 100) + (**20** + **90**) + (**3** + **4**) = **800** + **110** + **7** = **917**

P107 89, 99, 986, 979
97, 97, 98, 979, 778, 876

P108 142, 73, 105, 111, 35, 151, 120
Riverton has 155 third graders.

P109 881, 1,342, 764
1,194, 1,414, 680, 1,549
1,360, 1,178, 1,530, 895
365 people visited over the weekend.
Hannah and Luke raised $371.

P110 52 + 29 = (52 + **30**) − 1 = **82** − 1 = **81**
17 + 69 = (17 + **70**) − 1 = **87** − 1 = **86**
76 + 38 = (76 + **40**) − 2 = **116** − 2 = **114**
75 + 78 = (75 + **80**) − 2 = **155** − 2 = **153**
314 + 299 = (314 + **300**) − 1 = **614** − 1 = **613**
146 + 699 = (146 + **700**) − 1 = **846** − 1 = **845**
425 + 398 = (425 + **400**) − 2 = **825** − 2 = **823**
244 + 599 = (244 + **600**) − 1 = **844** − 1 = **843**

P111 27, 27, 28
28, 63, 8, 7
29 children will need to wait.

P112 249, 225, 448
207, 227, 89, 171
170, 872, 7, 107
68 people made it to the next round.
207 children stopped taking art classes.

P113 Owen needs to save an extra $18.
1,010 people traveled to Sun Island.
Mila picked 72 plums over the weekend.
Hailey's second score was 78 points higher than her first score. $99 + $45 = (100 + 45) − 1 = 145 − 1 = $144

P114

problem	**estimation**
31 + 54 = **85**	30 + 54 = **84**
399 + 466 = **865**	400 + 466 = **866**
502 + 264 = **766**	500 + 264 = **764**
601 + 385 = **986**	600 + 385 = **985**
198 + 727 = **925**	200 + 727 = **927**
estimation	**problem**
$100 + $34 = $134	$99 + $34 = $133

There is a $1 difference between the estimation and the actual price.

P115

problem	**estimation**
74 − 29 = **45**	74 − 30 = **44**
526 − 301 = **225**	526 − 300 = **226**
482 − 198 = **284**	482 − 200 = **282**
724 − 502 = **222**	724 − 500 = **224**
963 − 599 = **364**	963 − 600 = **363**
estimation	**problem**
$54 − $30 = $24	$54 − $29 = $25

P116 98, 91, 132
642, 529, 756, 448
876, 593, 696, 1,749
1,532, 1,579

P117
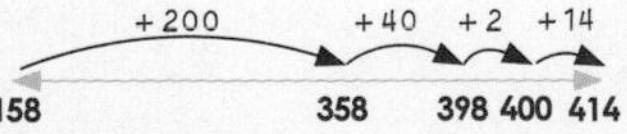

+ 200
+ 40
+ 2
+ 14
158
358
398 400 414

414 − 158 = 256

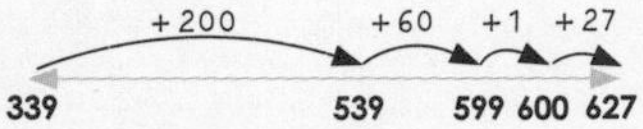

+ 200
+ 60
+ 1
+ 27
339
539
599 600 627

627 − 339 = 288

+ 400
+ 5
+ 1
525
925
930
931

931 − 525 = 406

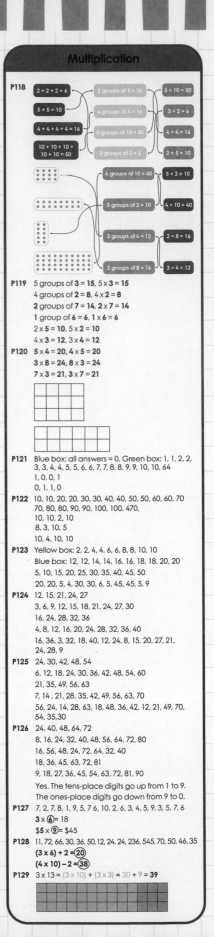

Multiplication

P118
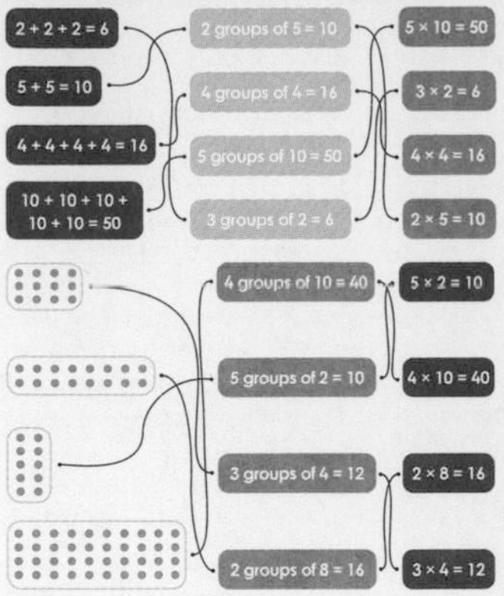

2 + 2 + 2 = 6
5 + 5 = 10
4 + 4 + 4 + 4 = 16
10 + 10 + 10 + 10 + 10 = 50
2 groups of 5 = 10
4 groups of 4 = 16
5 groups of 10 = 50
3 groups of 2 = 6
5 × 10 = 50
3 × 2 = 6
4 × 4 = 16
2 × 5 = 10
4 groups of 10 = 40
5 groups of 2 = 10
3 groups of 4 = 12
2 groups of 8 = 16
5 × 2 = 10
4 × 10 = 40
2 × 8 = 16
3 × 4 = 12

P119 5 groups of **3** = **15**, 5 x **3** = **15**
4 groups of **2** = **8**, 4 x **2** = **8**
2 groups of **7** = **14**, **2** x **7** = **14**
1 group of **6** = **6**, **1** x **6** = **6**
2 x **5** = **10**, 5 x **2** = **10**
4 x **3** = **12**, 3 x **4** = **12**

P120 **5** x **4** = **20**, **4** x **5** = **20**
3 x **8** = **24**, **8** x **3** = **24**
7 x **3** = **21**, **3** x **7** = **21**
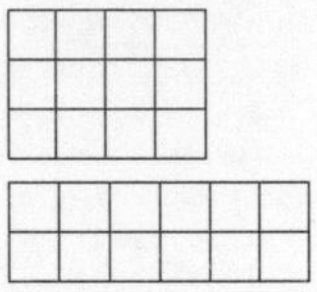

P121 Blue box: all answers = 0. Green box: 1, 1, 2, 2, 3, 3, 4, 4, 5, 5, 6, 6, 7, 7, 8, 8, 9, 9, 10, 10, 64
1, 0, 0, 1
0, 1, 1, 0

P122 10, 10, 20, 20, 30, 30, 40, 40, 50, 50, 60, 60, 70 70, 80, 80, 90, 90, 100, 100, 470,
10, 10, 2, 10
8, 3, 10, 5
10, 4, 10, 10

P123 Yellow box: 2, 2, 4, 4, 6, 6, 8, 8, 10, 10
Blue box: 12, 12, 14, 14, 16, 16, 18, 18, 20, 20
5, 10, 15, 20, 25, 30, 35, 40, 45, 50
20, 20, 5, 4, 30, 30, 6, 5, 45, 45, 5, 9

P124 12, 15, 21, 24, 27
3, 6, 9, 12, 15, 18, 21, 24, 27, 30
16, 24, 28, 32, 36
4, 8, 12, 16, 20, 24, 28, 32, 36, 40
16, 36, 3, 32, 18, 40, 12, 24, 8, 15, 20, 27, 21, 24, 28, 9

P125 24, 30, 42, 48, 54
6, 12, 18, 24, 30, 36, 42, 48, 54, 60
21, 35, 49, 56, 63
7, 14, 21, 28, 35, 42, 49, 56, 63, 70
56, 24, 14, 28, 63, 18, 48, 36, 42, 12, 21, 49, 70, 54, 35,30

P126 24, 40, 48, 64, 72
8, 16, 24, 32, 40, 48, 56, 64, 72, 80
16, 56, 48, 24, 72, 64, 32, 40
18, 36, 45, 63, 72, 81
9, 18, 27, 36, 45, 54, 63, 72, 81, 90
Yes. The tens-place digits go up from 1 to 9. The ones-place digits go down from 9 to 0.

P127 7, 2, 7, 8, 1, 9, 5, 7, 6, 10, 2, 6, 3, 4, 5, 9, 3, 5, 7, 6
3 x (**6**) = 18
$5 x (**9**) = $45

P128 11, 72, 66, 30, 36, 50, 12, 24, 24, 236, 545, 70, 50, 46, 35
(3 x 6) + 2 = (**20**)
(4 x 10) − 2 = (**38**)

P129 3 x 13 = (3 x 10) + (3 x 3) = 30 + 9 = **39**
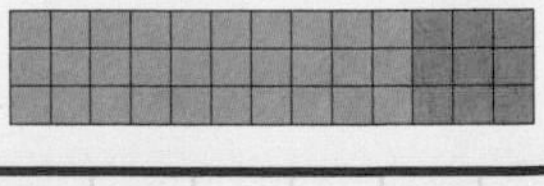

$5 \times 15 = (5 \times 10) + (5 \times 5) = 50 + 25 = 75$

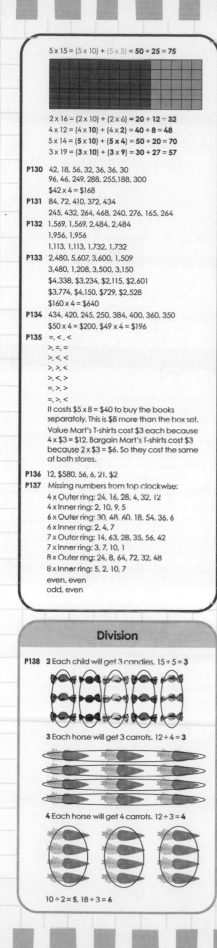

$2 \times 16 = (2 \times 10) + (2 \times 6) = 20 + 12 = 32$
$4 \times 12 = (4 \times 10) + (4 \times 2) = 40 + 8 = 48$
$5 \times 14 = (5 \times 10) + (5 \times 4) = 50 + 20 = 70$
$3 \times 19 = (3 \times 10) + (3 \times 9) = 30 + 27 = 57$

P130 42, 18, 56, 32, 36, 36, 30
96, 46, 249, 288, 255,188, 300
$42 \times 4 = \$168$

P131 84, 72, 410, 372, 434
245, 432, 264, 468, 240, 276, 165, 264

P132 1,569, 1,569, 2,484, 2,484
1,956, 1,956
1,113, 1,113, 1,732, 1,732

P133 2,480, 5,607, 3,600, 1,509
3,480, 1,208, 3,500, 3,150
$4,338, $3,234, $2,115, $2,601
$3,774, $4,150, $729, $2,528
$160 \times 4 = \$640$

P134 434, 420, 245, 250, 384, 400, 360, 350
$50 \times 4 = \$200$, $49 \times 4 = \$196$

P135 =, <, <
>, =, =
>, <, <
>, >, <
>, <, >
=, >, >
=, >, <
It costs $5 \times 8 = \$40$ to buy the books
separately. This is $8 more than the box set.
Value Mart's T-shirts cost $3 each because
$4 \times \$3 = \$12$. Bargain Mart's T-shirts cost $3
because $2 \times \$3 = \$6$. So they cost the same
at both stores.

P136 12, $580, 56, 6, 21, $2

P137 Missing numbers from top clockwise:
4 × Outer ring: 24, 16, 28, 4, 32, 12
4 × Inner ring: 2, 10, 9, 5
6 × Outer ring: 30, 48, 60, 18, 54, 36, 6
6 × Inner ring: 2, 4, 7
7 × Outer ring: 14, 63, 28, 35, 56, 42
7 × Inner ring: 3, 7, 10, 1
8 × Outer ring: 24, 8, 64, 72, 32, 48
8 × Inner ring: 5, 2, 10, 7
even, even
odd, even

Division

P138 **2** Each child will get 3 candies. $15 \div 5 = 3$

3 Each horse will get 3 carrots. $12 \div 4 = 3$

4 Each horse will get 4 carrots. $12 \div 3 = 4$

$10 \div 2 = 5$, $18 \div 3 = 6$

P139

It took **3** jumps to reach 0. $18 \div 6 = 3$

It took **3** jumps to reach 0. $21 \div 7 = 3$

It took **4** jumps to reach 0. $20 \div 5 = 4$
0, 4, 0, 3, 0, 3

P140 24, 6, 21, 3
30, 30, 10, 3, 54, 54, 9, 6, 48, 48, 8, 6

P141 7, 7, 6, 6, 8, 8
9, 2, 4, 10, 1, 14, 8, 18
$8 \div 2 =$ ④

P142 4, 4, 8, 8, 5, 5, 6, 6
2, 10, 3, 7, 9, 1, 15, 9
$27 \div 3 =$ ⑨

P143 5, 5, 8, 8, 3, 3, 7, 7
2, 9, 4, 6, 1, 1, 10, 24, 32
$16 \div 4 =$ ④

P144 2, 2, 3, 3, 7, 7, 5, 5
9, 8, 6, 1, 4, 10, 20, 35
$30 \div 5 =$ ⑥

P145 3, 3, 4, 4, 6, 6, 7, 7
8, 1, 2, 10, 9, 5, 48, 54
$12 \div 6 =$ ②

P146 4, 4, 2, 2, 5, 5, 3, 3
7, 1, 6, 9, 10, 8, 28, 42
$56 \div 7 =$ ⑧

P147 3, 3, 2, 2, 5, 5, 4, 4
8, 7, 9, 6, 10, 1, 48, 8
$48 \div 8 =$ ⑥

P148 4, 4, 3, 3, 2, 2, 5, 5
1, 8, 9, 6, 10, 7, 36, 81
$72 \text{ m} \div 9 =$ **8 m**

P149 2, 8, 3, 5, 10, 4, 1, 7, 9, 6, 60, 100, 34, 48, 50, 320
28, 20, 72, 150
$500 \text{ cm} \div 10 =$ **50 cm**

P150 $4 \div 1 = 4$, $6 \div 1 = 6$
2, 6, 10, 17, 73, 1, 64, 37, 90, 60, 989, 7,336
$40 \text{ cm} \div 1 =$ **40 cm**

P151

6, 4, 4, 7, 7, 6, 9, 3
$15 \div 3 =$ ⑤ $24 \div 4 =$ ⑥

P152 13, 24, 23, 14, 14, 18, 21, 12
13, 43, 11, 15, 14, 27

P153 9, 40, 14, 10, 3, 10, 7, 20, 10, 255, 881, 53, 29,
36, 23, 20
$(16 \div 4) + (8 \div 4) = 6$
$(32 \div 4) + 2 = 10$

P154 <, >, <
>, =, =
=, <, =
<, <, =
>, >, >
>, =, >
<, >, >
$24 \div 3 = \$8$ The planes cost $8 each in a
bag of 3, and $9 each separately, so they're

each $1 cheaper in a bag of 3.
$14 \div 7 = \$2$ and $12 \div 4 = \$3$. The pens are $1
cheaper at Value Mart than at Bargain Mart.

P155 7, 32, 7, 43, 48, 10, 10, 9, 1, 16, 7, 24, 21, 9, 80, 1, 4,
27, 10, 4, 3, 20, 10, 1
$30 \div \$6 =$ ⑤
$$6 \overline{)90} \;\; 15$$

P156 13, 14, 13,
$(9 \div 3) + 2 = 5$
$(54 \div 6) - 1 = 8$
$$5 \overline{)100} \;\; 20$$

P157 $20 \times 3 = 60$, $60 \div 3 = 20$, $60 \div 20 = 3$
$4 \times 20 = 80$, $80 \div 4 = 20$, $80 \div 20 = 4$
$5 \times 20 = 100$, $100 \div 5 = 20$, $100 \div 20 = 5$
$25 \times 2 = 50$, $50 \div 2 = 25$, $50 \div 25 = 2$
$2 \times 40 = 80$, $80 \div 2 = 40$, $80 \div 40 = 2$
$3 \times 25 = 75$, $75 \div 3 = 25$, $75 \div 25 = 3$
$200 \times 10 = 2,000$, $2,000 \div 10 = 200$, $2,000 \div 200 = 10$
$38 \times 24 = 912$, $912 \div 24 = 38$, $912 \div 38 = 24$

Fractions and Decimals

P158 **2** All but the yellow-shaded circle have
exactly 1/2 shaded.
$6 \div 2 = 3$, $8 \div 2 = 4$

P159

3 All but the pink-shaded rectangle have
exactly 1/3 shaded.
$18 \div 3 = \$6$, $9 \div 3 = 3$

P160

4 All but the green-shaded square have
exactly 1/4 shaded.
Four quarters make one dollar. $25 \times 4 = 100$

P161 3/4, 3/6, 2/6

4/5, 3/6
5/8, 6/10, 1/9

P162 3/8, 4/10, 6/9, 2/6

4/7

P163 5, 5, 7, 7, 4, 4
3, 9, 8, 2, 3, 6, 7

P164 2/8 + 3/8 = 5/8, 2/4 + 1/4 = 3/4
4/10 + 5/10 = 9/10, 1/3 + 1/3 + 1/3 = 3/3

P165

1/4 + 1/4 = **2/4**   2/6 + 3/6 = **5/6**
4/5, 5/7, 2/2

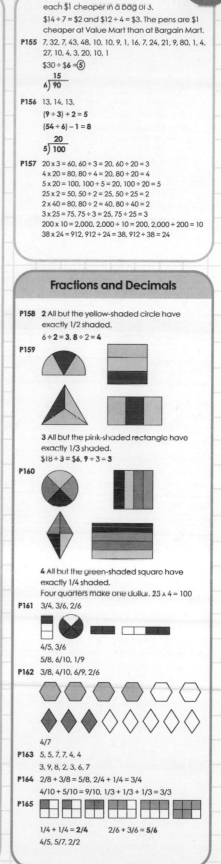

6/8, 2/9, 8/10
13/20, 11/12, 2/3
12/17, 27/30, 97/100

P166 7/10 – 3/10 = 4/10, 6/9 – 4/9 = 2/9, 5/6 – 2/6 = 3/6
1/7, 2/5, 1/3, 3/12, 4/10, 5/25, 5/6, 5/12, 10/40
30/100, 7/37, 15/67

P167 4/8, 2/4, 3/4, 1/2
All but the 3rd orange rectangle are equivalent fractions.
8/12, 4/6, 2/3, 1/3
All but the 4th blue circle down are equivalent fractions.
12/36, 6/18, 7/18
All but the 3rd pink rectangle down are equivalent fractions.

P168 3/6 < 4/6, 5/8 > 1/2, 2/5, 2/5 < 3/5, 1/2 = 2/4, 7/9 > 2/3, 4/8 = 2/4, 7/10 < 4/5, 4/6 = 2/3

P169 Hailey ate more pizza than Luke.
Noah had done more homework than Riley.
Zoe had eaten half of the candies. 5/10 = 1/2.

P170

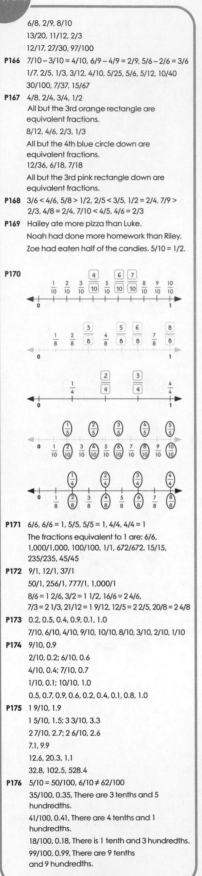

P171 6/6, 6/6 = 1, 5/5, 5/5 = 1, 4/4, 4/4 = 1
The fractions equivalent to 1 are: 6/6, 1,000/1,000, 100/100, 1/1, 672/672, 15/15, 235/235, 45/45

P172 9/1, 12/1, 37/1
50/1, 256/1, 777/1, 1,000/1
8/6 = 1 2/6, 3/2 = 1 1/2, 16/6 = 2 4/6,
7/3 = 2 1/3, 21/12 = 1 9/12, 12/5 = 2 2/5, 20/8 = 2 4/8

P173 0.2, 0.5, 0.4, 0.9, 0.1, 1.0
7/10, 6/10, 4/10, 9/10, 10/10, 8/10, 3/10, 2/10, 1/10

P174 9/10, 0.9
2/10, 0.2; 6/10, 0.6
4/10, 0.4; 7/10, 0.7
1/10, 0.1; 10/10, 1.0
0.5, 0.7, 0.9, 0.6, 0.2, 0.4, 0.1, 0.8, 1.0

P175 1 9/10, 1.9
1 5/10, 1.5; 3 3/10, 3.3
2 7/10, 2.7; 2 6/10, 2.6
7.1, 9.9
12.6, 20.3, 1.1
32.8, 102.5, 528.4

P176 5/10 = 50/100, 6/10 ≠ 62/100
35/100, 0.35, There are 3 tenths and 5 hundredths.
41/100, 0.41, There are 4 tenths and 1 hundredths.
18/100, 0.18, There is 1 tenth and 3 hundredths.
99/100, 0.99, There are 9 tenths and 9 hundredths.

P177

	hundreds	tens	ones	•	tenths	hundredths
527.08	5	2	7	•	0	8
6.20			6	•	2	0
367.12	3	6	7	•	1	2
808.44	8	0	8	•	4	4
67.28		6	7	•	2	8
8.24			8	•	2	4
300.30	3	0	0	•	3	0
69.07		6	9	•	0	7
636.63	6	3	6	•	6	3
238.92	2	3	8	•	9	2
36.73		3	6	•	7	3
1.10			1	•	1	0
562.26	5	6	2	•	2	6
999.09	9	9	9	•	0	9

P178 $36.57, $12.27, $59.40, $10.06
$12.45, $12.48, $12.50
$4.00, $4.02, $4.20
$5.99, $6.00, $6.99
$72.56, $72.57, $73.56
$55.99, $56.00, $56.99

P179 Sophy and her brother ate 2/10 + 1/10 of the cookies. This is 3/10.
10/10 – 3/10 = 7/10. This means 7/10 or 7 of the 10 cookies were left.
They washed the same number of dishes because 1/2 is equivalent to 2/4.
Aria paid 1 cent more than Caden.
100 pennies, or cents, is equal to $1.
Leo's score can be written as 8/10 or as 0.8.
Leah's score can be written as 82/100 or as 0.82.

Measurement

P180 4 cm, 5 cl, 3 cg
20 cm, 5 km, 6 m
4 kg, 30 l, 2 kl
35 cl
5,000 m

P181 fingernail: millimeters, pool: kiloliters, plane: kilograms, distance: kilometers, feather: milligrams, juice: milliliters

P182 200 ml, 175 ml
140 g, 45 g

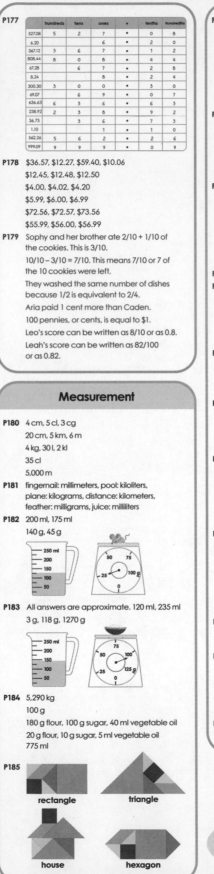

P183 All answers are approximate. 120 ml, 235 ml
3 g, 118 g, 1270 g

P184 5,290 kg
100 g
180 g flour, 100 g sugar, 40 ml vegetable oil
20 g flour, 10 g sugar, 5 ml vegetable oil
775 ml

P185

rectangle   triangle

house   hexagon

P186 square = all sides are the same length, and opposite sides are parallel; rectangle = opposite sides are the same length and parallel, trapezoid = only two sides are parallel.

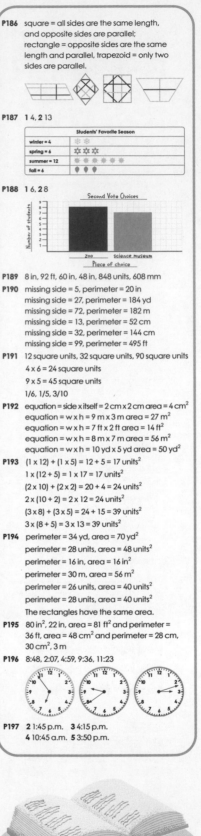

P187 1 4, 2 13

Students' Favorite Season	
winter = 4	❄ ❄
spring = 6	✿ ✿ ✿
summer = 12	☀ ☀ ☀ ☀ ☀ ☀
fall = 6	🍂 🍂 🍂

P188 1 6, 2 8

Second Vote Choices

P189 8 in, 92 ft, 60 in, 48 in, 848 units, 608 mm

P190 missing side = 5, perimeter = 20 in
missing side = 27, perimeter = 184 yd
missing side = 72, perimeter = 182 m
missing side = 13, perimeter = 52 cm
missing side = 32, perimeter = 144 cm
missing side = 99, perimeter = 495 ft

P191 12 square units, 32 square units, 90 square units
4 x 6 = 24 square units
9 x 5 = 45 square units
1/6, 1/5, 3/10

P192 equation = side x itself = 2 cm x 2 cm area = 4 cm^2
equation = w x h = 9 m x 3 m area = 27 m^2
equation = w x h = 7 ft x 2 ft area = 14 ft^2
equation = w x h = 8 m x 7 m area = 56 m^2
equation = w x h = 10 yd x 5 yd area = 50 yd^2

P193 (1 x 12) + (1 x 5) = 12 + 5 = 17 units^2
1 x (12 + 5) = 1 x 17 = 17 units^2
(2 x 10) + (2 x 2) = 20 + 4 = 24 units^2
2 x (10 + 2) = 2 x 12 = 24 units^2
(3 x 8) + (3 x 5) = 24 + 15 = 39 units^2
3 x (8 + 5) = 3 x 13 = 39 units^2

P194 perimeter = 34 yd, area = 70 yd^2
perimeter = 28 units, area = 48 units^2
perimeter = 16 in, area = 16 in^2
perimeter = 30 m, area = 56 m^2
perimeter = 26 units, area = 40 units^2
perimeter = 28 units, area = 40 units^2
The rectangles have the same area.

P195 80 in^2, 22 in, area = 81 ft^2 and perimeter = 36 ft, area = 48 cm^2 and perimeter = 28 cm, 30 cm^2, 3 m

P196 8:48, 2:07, 4:59, 9:36, 11:23

P197 2 1:45 p.m. 3 4:15 p.m.
4 10:45 a.m. 5 3:50 p.m.

Science and Technology

P198

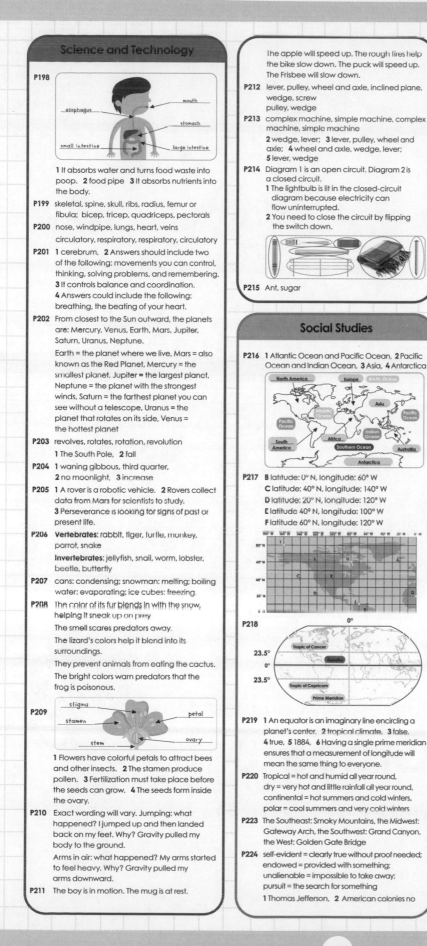

esophagus · mouth · stomach · small intestine · large intestine

1 It absorbs water and turns food waste into poop. **2** food pipe **3** It absorbs nutrients into the body.

P199 skeletal, spine, skull, ribs, radius, femur or fibula; bicep, tricep, quadriceps, pectorals

P200 nose, windpipe, lungs, heart, veins
circulatory, respiratory, respiratory, circulatory

P201 **1** cerebrum, **2** Answers should include two of the following: movements you can control, thinking, solving problems, and remembering. **3** It controls balance and coordination. **4** Answers could include the following: breathing, the beating of your heart.

P202 From closest to the Sun outward, the planets are: Mercury, Venus, Earth, Mars, Jupiter, Saturn, Uranus, Neptune.
Earth = the planet where we live, Mars = also known as the Red Planet, Mercury = the smallest planet, Jupiter = the largest planet, Neptune = the planet with the strongest winds, Saturn = the farthest planet you can see without a telescope, Uranus = the planet that rotates on its side, Venus = the hottest planet

P203 revolves, rotates, rotation, revolution
1 The South Pole, **2** fall

P204 **1** waning gibbous, third quarter, **2** no moonlight, **3** increase

P205 **1** A rover is a robotic vehicle. **2** Rovers collect data from Mars for scientists to study. **3** Perseverance is looking for signs of past or present life.

P206 **Vertebrates:** rabbit, tiger, turtle, monkey, parrot, snake
Invertebrates: jellyfish, snail, worm, lobster, beetle, butterfly

P207 cans: condensing; snowman: melting; boiling water: evaporating; ice cubes: freezing

P208 The color of its fur blends in with the snow, helping it sneak up on prey.
The smell scares predators away.
The lizard's colors help it blend into its surroundings.
They prevent animals from eating the cactus.
The bright colors warn predators that the frog is poisonous.

P209

stigma · petal · stamen · stem · ovary

1 Flowers have colorful petals to attract bees and other insects. **2** The stamen produce pollen. **3** Fertilization must take place before the seeds can grow. **4** The seeds form inside the ovary.

P210 Exact wording will vary. Jumping: what happened? I jumped up and then landed back on my feet. Why? Gravity pulled my body to the ground.
Arms in air: what happened? My arms started to feel heavy. Why? Gravity pulled my arms downward.

P211 The boy is in motion. The mug is at rest.

The apple will speed up. The rough tires help the bike slow down. The puck will speed up. The Frisbee will slow down.

P212 lever, pulley, wheel and axle, inclined plane, wedge, screw
pulley, wedge

P213 complex machine, simple machine, complex machine, simple machine
2 wedge, lever; **3** lever, pulley, wheel and axle; **4** wheel and axle, wedge, lever; **5** lever, wedge

P214 Diagram 1 is an open circuit. Diagram 2 is a closed circuit.
1 The lightbulb is lit in the closed-circuit diagram because electricity can flow uninterrupted.
2 You need to close the circuit by flipping the switch down.

P215 Ant, sugar

Social Studies

P216 **1** Atlantic Ocean and Pacific Ocean, **2** Pacific Ocean and Indian Ocean, **3** Asia, **4** Antarctica

North America · Europe · Arctic Ocean · Asia · Atlantic Ocean · Pacific Ocean · Pacific Ocean · South America · Africa · Indian Ocean · Southern Ocean · Australia · Antarctica

P217 **B** latitude: 0° N, longitude: 60° W
C latitude: 40° N, longitude: 140° W
D latitude: 20° N, longitude: 120° W
E latitude 40° N, longitude: 100° W
F latitude 60° N, longitude: 120° W

P218
0°
Tropic of Cancer
23.5°
0°
23.5°
Tropic of Capricorn
Prime Meridian

P219 **1** An equator is an imaginary line encircling a planet's center. **2** tropical climate, **3** false, **4** true, **5** 1884, **6** Having a single prime meridian ensures that a measurement of longitude will mean the same thing to everyone.

P220 Tropical = hot and humid all year round, dry = very hot and little rainfall all year round, continental = hot summers and cold winters, polar = cool summers and very cold winters

P223 The Southeast: Smoky Mountains, the Midwest: Gateway Arch, the Southwest: Grand Canyon, the West: Golden Gate Bridge

P224 self-evident = clearly true without proof needed; endowed = provided with something; unalienable = impossible to take away; pursuit = the search for something
1 Thomas Jefferson, **2** American colonies no

longer wanted to be ruled by the King of England. They wanted their independence.

p225 **1** republic, **2** Bill of Rights, **3** 1787

R	M	A	D	X	O	A	N	M	L	M	I	N	T	U
E	V	C	I	A	V	W	R	A	Q	M	E	T	Y	W
P	R	U	L	G	M	I	B	D	E	O	N	O	C	E
U	G	I	C	O	N	S	T	I	T	U	T	I	O	N
B	L	O	H	V	C	T	R	S	L	P	X	Y	N	J
L	U	G	V	R	E	E	O	O	S	D	A	I	S	O
I	O	S	C	E	B	A	T	N	B	E	P	B	T	L
C	S	A	U	D	R	T	L	P	U	E	V	H	G	T
E	R	L	M	B	L	N	Y	I	C	F	K	N	W	A
O	W	K	A	G	O	V	M	C	I	S	Q	U	N	Z
A	F	C	D	Z	E	J	R	E	P	U	N	I	O	A
H	J	A	I	I	N	E	U	A	N	E	O	R	I	U
B	I	L	L	O	F	R	I	G	H	T	S	B	U	E

P226 **1** Legislative Branch, Executive Branch, Judicial Branch, **2** the President of the United States, **3** the US Senate and the US House of Representatives, **4** The Judicial Branch interprets the laws.

P228 **Citizens' rights:** the right to vote, to run for public office, to hold most government jobs, to run for president. **Non-American citizens' rights:** to have a driver's license, buy a house, have a job.
False, false

P229 **1** the Mohawk, Oneida, Onondaga, Cayuga, Seneca, and Tuscarora, **2** in the eastern Great Lakes region, **3** They lived in extended families, related on the mother's side. **4** corn, beans, and squash

P230 **1** present-day South Carolina, North Carolina, Georgia, and Tennessee, **2** thin branches and mud, **3** corn, beans, squash, fish, and animals they hunted **4** The Cherokee people were forced to leave their homes, and more than 4,000 people died on the march west.

P231 **1** the Dakota, Lakota, and Nakota speaking peoples, **2** Nomadic means people who move to follow their main food source. **3** They used the bison to make their clothing, tools, and shelter. **4** They were two of many Lakota Sioux chiefs who fought against the US government takeover of their lands.

P232 **1** 3, 1, 2, **2** 1876 **3** the Cherokee Trail of Tears **4** 78 years

p233 Answers may vary. **Abigail Adams:** second first lady, first lady from 1797 until 1801, believed in equal education for all; **Eleanor Roosevelt:** thirty-second first lady, first lady during the Great Depression from 1933 until 1945, campaigned for civil rights and worker's rights; **both:** first ladies of the United States of America, worked closely with their husbands to better human rights, cared about women's rights.

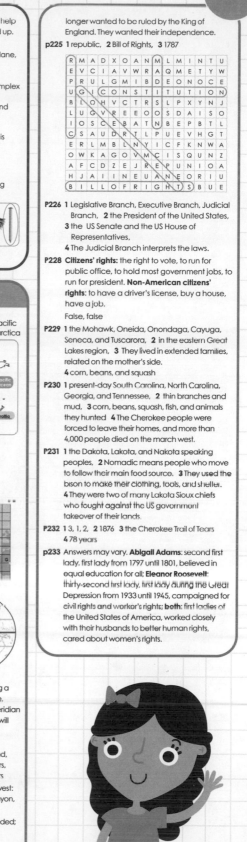

Congratulations!

Good Work Award!

Name: _____

has successfully completed the

Grade 3

Jumbo Workbook

Date: _____